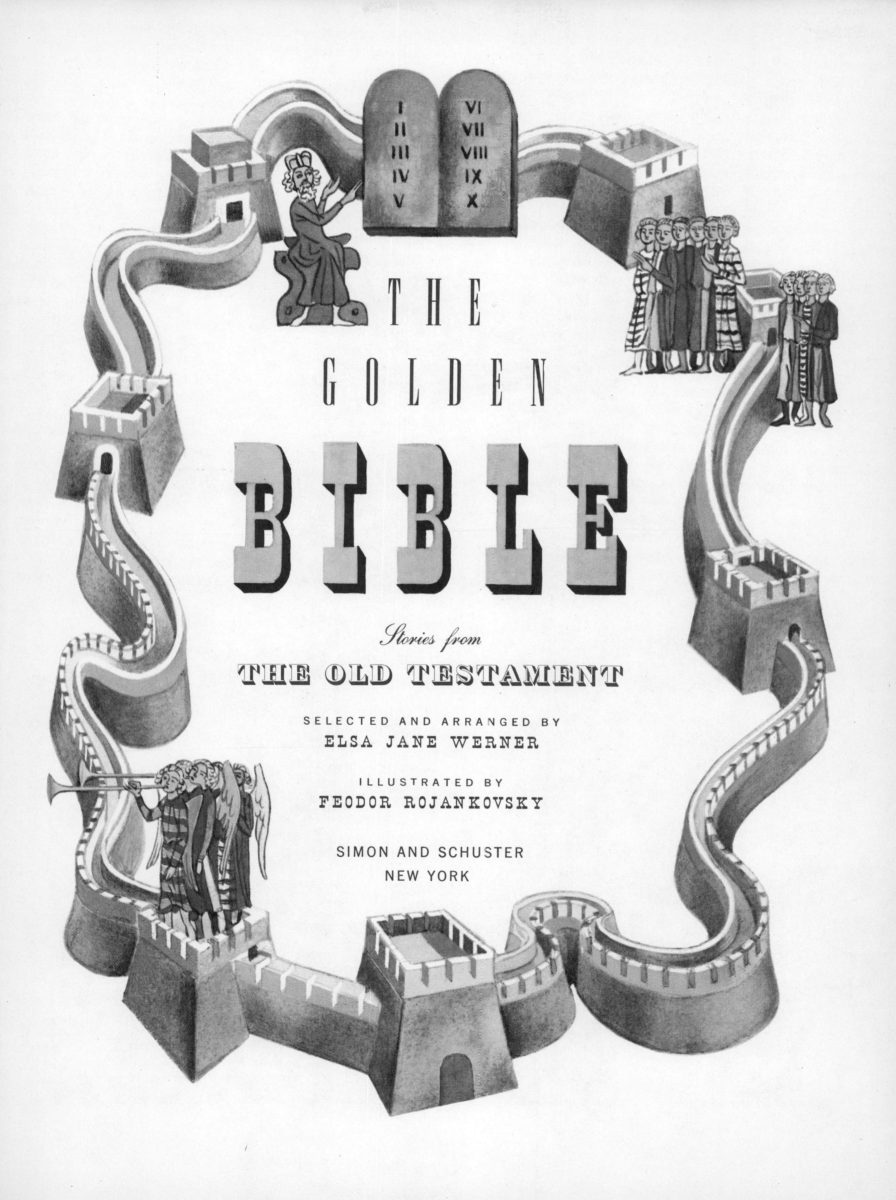

THE GOLDEN BIBLE

Stories from
THE OLD TESTAMENT

SELECTED AND ARRANGED BY
ELSA JANE WERNER

ILLUSTRATED BY
FEODOR ROJANKOVSKY

SIMON AND SCHUSTER
NEW YORK

CONTENTS

	Page		Page
THE CREATION OF THE WORLD	8	JACOB AND ESAU AND THE BIRTHRIGHT	23
THE GARDEN OF EDEN	10	JACOB TRICKS HIS FATHER	24
THE SERPENT IN THE GARDEN	11	JACOB'S DREAM IN THE DESERT	26
CAIN AND ABEL, SONS OF ADAM	12	JACOB AND RACHEL	28
NOAH AND THE GREAT FLOOD	13	JOSEPH IS SOLD INTO SLAVERY	29
THE TOWER OF BABEL	16	JOSEPH IN THE LAND OF EGYPT	31
ABRAM AND LOT SEEK NEW PASTURES	18	JOSEPH'S BROTHERS IN EGYPT	36
ABRAHAM AND THE ANGELS	19	BENJAMIN GOES TO EGYPT	38
CHOOSING A WIFE FOR ISAAC	20	MOSES IN THE BULRUSHES	45

	Page		Page
MOSES IN EXILE	47	DAVID AND GOLIATH	87
MOSES AND THE BURNING BUSH	48	THE FRIENDSHIP OF DAVID AND JONATHAN	89
THE PLAGUES OF EGYPT	51	DAVID SPARES SAUL'S LIFE	91
THE NIGHT OF THE PASSOVER	55	THE PSALMS OF DAVID	92
CROSSING THE RED SEA	56	THE WISDOM OF SOLOMON	94
THE BITTER WELL OF MARAH	60	SOLOMON BUILDS THE TEMPLE	96
MANNA FROM HEAVEN	61	ELIJAH AND THE POOR WIDOW	96
THE TEN COMMANDMENTS	63	ELIJAH AND THE PRIESTS OF BAAL	98
AARON MAKES THE GOLDEN CALF	66	THE PARTING OF ELIJAH AND ELISHA	100
THE PROMISED LAND	68	ELISHA CURES NAAMAN'S LEPROSY	102
MOSES COMPLETES HIS WORK	70	THE PROPHECY OF ISAIAH	103
JOSHUA SENDS SPIES INTO CANAAN	70	JOSIAH AND THE BOOK OF THE LAW	104
THE FALL OF JERICHO	72	JERUSALEM IS DESTROYED	106
GIDEON AND THE MIDIANITES	74	THE SONG OF THE CAPTIVES	107
THE TRUMPETS AND THE LAMPS	74	DANIEL AT NEBUCHADNEZZAR'S COURT	108
THE PARABLE OF THE TREES	76	THE STATUE OF GOLD	110
SAMSON AND HIS MIGHTY STRENGTH	77	THE HANDWRITING ON THE WALL	114
RUTH, THE FAITHFUL DAUGHTER-IN-LAW	80	DANIEL IN THE LIONS' DEN	117
SAMUEL, CHILD OF THE LORD	83	THE TEMPLE IS REBUILT	120
DAVID, THE LORD'S CHOSEN ONE	85	ESTHER SAVES HER PEOPLE	121
DAVID MEETS SAUL THE KING	86		

THE CREATION OF THE WORLD

THE FIRST DAY

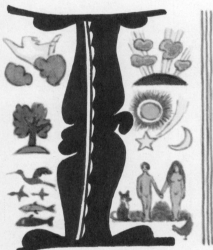

IN THE beginning God created the heavens and the earth. But the earth was empty, and there was a great darkness everywhere.

Then God said, "Let there be light," and there was light. He called the light Day and the darkness Night.

THE SECOND DAY

God said, "Let there be a sky to divide the waters below from the waters above." God made the sky and called it Heaven.

THE THIRD DAY

"Let the waters be gathered together and let dry land appear," said God. And so it was. God called the dry land Earth, and the waters he called Seas.

Then God said, "Let the earth bring forth grass, herbs, and fruit trees." And the earth brought them forth.

THE FOURTH DAY

God said, "Let there be lights in the sky to give light to the earth." He made two great lights, the greater to rule the day, and the lesser to rule the night, and he made the stars also.

THE FIFTH DAY

"Let the waters bring forth living, moving creatures, many of them, and let birds fly in the heavens," said God. Then he created great whales and every living creature of the waters, and every winged bird, and he blessed them all.

THE SIXTH DAY

God said, "Let the earth bring forth living creatures of all kinds, cattle and creeping things and beasts of the earth." He made the beasts of the earth, and the cattle, and everything that creeps upon the earth.

Then God said, "Let us make man in our image, and let him have power over the fish of the sea and over the birds of the air, and over the cattle, and over all the earth and everything that creeps upon the earth."

So God created man in his own image; male and female he created. And God blessed them and gave them dominion over the whole world.

Then God looked at everything he had made, and he saw that it was good.

THE SEVENTH DAY

Thus the heavens and the earth were finished and filled with life. And on the seventh day God rested from his work. God blessed the seventh day and made it holy because on that day he had rested.

THE GARDEN OF EDEN

THE LORD GOD formed man of the dust of the ground and into his nostrils he breathed the breath of life, and man became a living soul.

And then the Lord God planted a garden eastward in Eden, and there he put the man whom he had made. Out of the ground the Lord made to grow every tree that is pleasant to look at and good for food. The tree of life also grew in the midst of the garden, and the tree of knowledge of good and evil.

The Lord took the man, and put him into the garden of Eden to dress it and to keep it. And the Lord God commanded the man, saying, "Of every tree in the garden you may eat freely, but of the tree of the knowledge of good and evil do not eat. For in the day that you eat of it you will surely die."

The Lord God brought every beast of the field and every fowl of the air which he had made out of the earth to Adam to see what he would call them. Whatever Adam called each living creature became that creature's name. Adam gave names to all cattle, and to the birds of the air, and to every beast of the field, but for Adam himself there still was no helpmeet.

The Lord God said, "It is not good that the man should be alone. I will make a helpmeet for him."

Then the Lord God caused a deep sleep to fall upon Adam. As Adam slept the Lord took one of his ribs, and filled its place with flesh. This rib the Lord God made into a woman, and he brought her to the man.

Adam said, "This is now bone of my bones and flesh of my flesh. She shall be called Woman, because she was taken out of Man."

THE SERPENT IN THE GARDEN

NOW the serpent was the most cunning beast which the Lord had made. He said to the woman, "Has not God told you that you may eat of every tree in the garden?"

"We may eat of the fruit of the trees of the garden," said the woman, "but of the fruit of the tree which is in the middle of the garden, God has said, 'You shall not eat of it nor touch it, lest you die.'"

"You would not die," said the serpent, "for God knows that the day you eat of that fruit your eyes will be opened, and you will be like gods, knowing good from evil."

When the woman saw that the tree was good for food, and that it was pleasant to the eyes, and a tree to be desired because it could make one wise, she picked some of the fruit and ate it. She gave it to her husband, and he also ate it.

Then their eyes were opened, and they realized that they were naked, and they sewed fig leaves together to cover themselves.

They heard the voice of the Lord God walking in the garden in the cool of the day; and Adam and his wife hid themselves from the sight of the Lord, among the trees of the garden.

The Lord God called to Adam, saying, "Where are you?"

"I heard your voice in the garden," said Adam, "and I was afraid because I was naked, and I hid myself."

"Who told you that you were naked?" asked the Lord God. "Have you eaten of the tree whose fruit I commanded you not to eat?"

Adam said, "The woman whom you gave me to be with me, she gave me the fruit, and I ate."

Then the Lord God said to the woman, "What is this you have done?"

And the woman said, "The serpent tempted me, and I ate."

Then the Lord God said to the serpent, "Because you have done this, you are cursed above all cattle and above every beast of the field. You shall crawl on your belly and eat dust all the days of your life. I shall make the woman and her children enemies of you and of your children through the years. They shall bruise your head, and you shall bruise their heel."

To the woman he said, "I will multiply your suffering. In sorrow you shall bring forth your children. You shall depend on your husband for happiness, and he shall rule over you."

To Adam he said, "Because you listened to your wife and ate of the forbidden fruit, the ground shall be cursed for you; in sorrow you shall eat of it all the days of your life. Thorns and thistles it will bring forth for you, and you will have to eat wild grasses of the field. By the sweat of your brow you will earn your bread until you return to the earth."

The Lord God then made coats of skin for Adam and his wife, and dressed them.

And the Lord God said, "The man is like one of us now, knowing good and evil. Now if he were to put out his hand and eat also of the tree of life, he would live forever."

Therefore the Lord God sent Adam out of the garden of Eden, to till the ground from which he was made. He drove the man out, and placed at the east of the garden of Eden cherubims, and a flaming sword which turned in every direction to guard the path to the tree of life.

CAIN AND ABEL, SONS OF ADAM

ADAM called his wife Eve, because she was the mother of all. First she bore Cain, and said, "I have gotten a man from the Lord." Later she bore Abel. Abel was a keeper of sheep, but Cain was a tiller of the ground. And it came to pass one day that Cain brought the fruit of his harvest as an offering to the Lord. And Abel also brought some of the young of his flock, the best of them all. Now the Lord had respect for Abel and his offering, but for Cain and his offering he had no respect. Cain was very angry, and his face fell.

The Lord said to Cain, "Why are you angry? Why has your face fallen? If you do well, shall you not be accepted?"

Cain talked with Abel, his brother. And it came to pass, when they were in the field, that Cain rose up against Abel his brother and killed him.

The Lord said to Cain, "Where is Abel, your brother?"

And he said, "How should I know? Am I my brother's keeper?"

"What have you done?" said the Lord. "The voice of your brother's blood cries to me from the ground. And now you are cursed from the earth, which has received your brother's blood from your hand. Henceforth when you till the ground, it will not yield you its best. A fugitive and a vagabond you shall be in the earth."

Cain said to the Lord, "My punishment is greater than I can bear. Behold, you have driven me out this day from the face of the earth, and from your face I shall be hid. I shall be a fugitive and a vagabond in the earth. Everyone who finds me will want to kill me."

The Lord said to him, "Whoever kills Cain, revenge shall be taken on him seven times over." And the Lord set a mark upon Cain, so that anyone finding him would not kill him.

Then Cain went out from the presence of the Lord, and dwelt in the Land of Nod, on the east of Eden.

NOAH AND THE GREAT FLOW

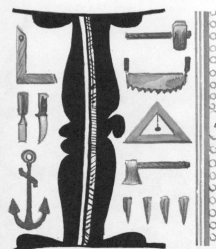

IT CAME to pass, when men began to multiply on the face of the earth, that God saw that the wickedness of man was great, and that every thought of his heart was evil. Then the Lord regretted that he had made man live on the earth, and he grieved in his heart.

The Lord said, "I will destroy man, whom I have created, from the face of the earth, both man and beast and the creeping things and the birds of the air, for I am sorry I made them."

Only Noah found approval in the eyes of the Lord.

Noah was a just man, the best of all the men of his time, and Noah lived by God's rules. He had three sons, named Shem, Ham, and Japheth.

God said to Noah, "I will destroy all living things on the earth, for the earth is filled with evil because of them.

"Make an ark of oleander wood. Make rooms in the ark, and cover it with pitch within and without. And this is the shape which you shall make it: the length of the ark shall be four hundred fifty feet, the breadth of it seventy-five feet, and the height of it forty-five feet. You shall make a window in the ark. Put a door in the side of the ark, and make three stories in it.

"I will bring a flood of waters upon the earth to destroy all flesh under heaven that has the breath of life. And every thing that is on the earth shall die.

"But with you I will establish a covenant, and you shall come into the ark, and your sons, and your wife and your sons' wives with you.

"And of every living thing, two of each sort you shall bring into the ark to keep them alive with you. They shall be male and female. Birds of all kinds, and cattle of all kinds, creeping things of all kinds—two of every kind of creature shall come to you to keep them alive.

"Take up, too, some of every kind of food that is eaten, and gather it up. And it shall be food for you and for them."

All this Noah did, just as God commanded him.

Noah was six hundred years old when the flood of waters came upon the earth. He went into the ark, with his sons, and his wife, and his sons' wives, because of the waters of the flood. And two by two the beasts and birds and every thing that creeps upon the earth went into the Ark, a male and female of each kind, as God had commanded Noah.

The same day all the fountains of the great deep were broken up, and the windows of heaven were opened. The rain fell upon the

earth forty days and forty nights. The waters increased, and bore up the ark, and it was lifted up above the earth. The waters spread out and increased still more, and the ark floated upon the face of the waters. The waters continued to rise all over the earth, and all the high hills under heaven were covered. Forty-five feet more the waters rose, and the mountains were covered.

Every living creature that moved upon the earth was destroyed, both man and cattle and the creeping things and the birds of the heavens.

Noah alone remained alive, and those who were with him in the ark. And the waters remained upon the earth a hundred and fifty days.

God remembered Noah and every living creature with him in the ark. God made a wind to pass over the earth, and the waters began to go down.

The fountains of the deep and the windows of heaven were stopped, and the rain from heaven was held back. The waters went down, day after day, for a hundred and fifty days.

In the seventh month, on the seventeenth day of the month, the ark rested upon the mountain of Ararat. In the tenth month, on the first day, the tops of the mountains were seen.

Then Noah opened the window which he had made in the ark, and he sent out a dove to see if the waters had dried from the face of the earth. But the dove found no rest for the sole of her foot, and she returned to the ark, for the waters covered the face of the whole earth. Then Noah put out his hand and took her back into the ark.

He waited seven days, and once again he sent the dove out of the ark. In the evening the dove came in to him, and in her mouth was a green olive leaf. So Noah knew that the waters were lowered on the face of the earth.

Seven more days Noah waited, and then once again he sent out the dove. She did not return to the ark any more.

So it came about that the waters were dried up from the earth, and Noah removed the cover of the ark and looked out, and behold, the ground was dry

God spoke to Noah, saying, "Go out of the ark and take every living creature that is with you, all the birds and animals and creeping things, that they may raise their young and multiply upon the earth."

15

Noah went out, and his sons and his wife and his sons' wives went with him. Every beast, every creeping thing, and every bird went out of the ark, too. And Noah built an altar to the Lord and offered up burnt offerings of every clean beast and every clean fowl.

The Lord smelled the sweet odor and said in his heart, "I will not curse the ground any more for man's sake; neither will I ever again strike down every living thing, as I have done. While the earth remains, seedtime and harvest, and cold and heat, summer and winter, and day and night shall not cease."

And God spoke to Noah, and to his sons with him, saying, "Behold, I establish my covenant with you, and with your children after you, and with every living creature that is with you, the birds, the cattle, and every beast of the earth, with all who come out of the ark. Never again will all flesh be cut off by the waters of a flood, nor will a flood destroy the earth.

"This is the token of the covenant which I make between myself and you and every creature that is with you, through generations without end. I set my rainbow in the cloud, and it shall be a token of the covenant between me and the earth.

"And it shall come to pass, when I bring a cloud over the earth, that the rainbow shall be seen in the cloud. I will look upon it, and I will remember the everlasting covenant between God and every living creature upon the earth."

THE TOWER OF BABEL

SONS were born unto the sons of Noah after the flood and they went forth and were the fathers of the nations of the earth. The whole earth then was of one language and had one speech.

WHEN the sons of Noah journeyed from the east, they found a plain in the land of Shinar, and they dwelt there.

Then they said one to another, "Come now, let us make bricks and burn them thoroughly." Soon they had brick for stone and slime for mortar.

Then they said, "Come now, let us build a city, and a tower whose top may reach up to heaven. Let us make a name for ourselves, lest we be scattered over the face of the whole earth."

The Lord came down to see the city and the tower which the children of men built. And the Lord said, "Behold, the people of the earth are one people and have one language, and this is just the beginning for them. Now nothing will be too much for them to attempt.

"Let us go down and confuse their language, so that they may not understand one another's speech."

And the Lord did as he promised, and scattered the people abroad over all the face of

the earth, and they left off building the city.
  Therefore the name of the place is called
Babel, because it was there that the Lord made a confusion of all the languages of the earth, and
it was from there that the Lord scattered the
people over all the face of the earth.

ABRAM AND LOT SEEK NEW PASTURES

BRAM was a man who lived in Haran. One day the Lord said to Abram, "Leave your country and your kinfolk, and your father's house, and go to a land that I will show you. I will make of you a great nation, and I will bless you and make your name great. I will bless those who bless you, and curse whoever curses you, and through you shall all the families of the earth be blessed."

So Abram departed, as the Lord had told him. He took Sarai his wife, and Lot his brother's son, and all their goods, and the people they had gathered in Haran, and they went forth into the land of Canaan.

Abram passed through this land to Sichem, on the plain of Moreh.

There the Lord appeared to Abram and said, "To your children I will give this land." And Abram built an altar to the Lord. Then Abram moved on to a mountain on the east of Bethel, and pitched his tent, having Bethel on the west and Hai on the east, and there he built an altar to the Lord and called upon the name of the Lord.

Abram was very rich in cattle and in silver and in gold.

Lot, who traveled with Abram, also had flocks and herds and tents, and the land was not able to support them all so that they could live together. There was trouble between the herdsmen of Abram's cattle and the herdsmen of Lot's cattle; and there were Canaanites and Perizzites, too, getting a living from the land.

Abram said to Lot, "Let us not have trouble, I beg of you, between me and you, nor between my herdsmen and your herdsmen, for we are brothers.

"Is not the whole land before us? Then let us separate, I beg you. If you will take the left hand, then I will go to the right. Or if you move to the right hand, then I will go to the left."

Lot lifted up his eyes, and looked out over all the plain of Jordan. He saw that it was well watered everywhere, like the garden of the Lord, and like the land of Egypt as you come to Zoar.

So Lot chose for himself all the plain of Jordan, and he journeyed east; and they separated one from the other.

So Abram lived in the land of Canaan, and Lot lived in the cities of the plain and pitched his tent near Sodom.

And the Lord said to Abram, after Lot had left him, "Lift up your eyes now, and look northward and southward, eastward and westward. For all the land which you see I will give to you and to your family for ever. And I will make your children's children as the dust of the earth, so that if a man could count the dust of the earth, he would also be able to count your children.

"Arise, walk through the land, the length of it and the breadth of it, for I will give it unto you."

ABRAHAM AND THE ANGELS

 OW when Abram was ninety-nine years old, the Lord appeared to him and said, "I am the Almighty God; walk in my ways and be perfect. I will make my covenant with you, and will make you the father of a great race. Your name shall be Abraham, and your wife's name Sarah, for I have made you a father of many nations."

Abraham bowed down to the ground, and God talked with him.

The Lord appeared to him again on the plains of Mamre as Abraham sat in the tent door in the heat of the day. And when Abraham lifted up his eyes and looked, lo, three men stood before him. He bowed himself toward the ground.

"My Lords," he said, "if I have now found favor in your sight, do not pass away, I beg you, from your servant. Let a little water be fetched, and wash your feet, and rest yourselves under the tree. I will bring bread to refresh you, and then you may go on your way."

And they said, "Do as you have said."

Abraham hastened into the tent where Sarah his wife was and said, "Make ready quickly three measures of fine meal, knead it, and make cakes upon the hearth."

Then he ran to the herd and fetched a calf, tender and good, and gave it to a young man to prepare.

Abraham then took butter and milk, and the calf, and set the food before the men. And he stood by them under the tree while they ate.

"Where is Sarah, your wife?" they asked him.

And he said, "See there, in the tent."

One of the men said, "Lo, Sarah your wife shall have a son."

Sarah heard this, standing in the tent doorway behind him. Now Abraham and Sarah were old and well along in years and they were beyond the time for having children. Therefore Sarah laughed within herself.

Then the Lord said to Abraham, "Why did Sarah laugh, saying she is too old to have a child? Is anything too hard for the Lord? At the time appointed Sarah shall have a son."

Then Sarah denied it, saying, "I did not laugh," for she was afraid.

But the Lord said, "No, you did laugh."

Then the men rose up and looked off toward Sodom, and Abraham went with them to put them on the right path.

And the Lord did as he had promised, and Sarah bore Abraham a son in his old age, at the set time of which God had spoken to him. And Abraham called the son Isaac.

CHOOSING A WIFE FOR ISAAC

YEARS later, Abraham was old and well along in age, and the Lord had blessed Abraham in all things. One day Abraham said to his eldest servant, who managed all that he had:

"Give me your hand, I pray you, and I will make you swear by the Lord, the God of heaven, and the God of earth, that you will not choose a wife for my son of the daughters of the Canaanites, among whom I dwell. But you shall go to my country and to my kindred and choose a wife for my son Isaac."

"Perhaps the woman will not be willing to follow me to this land," said the servant. "Must I take your son back again to the land from which you came?"

Abraham said to him, "Be sure that you do not take my son there again. The Lord God of heaven, who took me from my father's house and from the land of my kindred, spoke to me and promised, saying, 'To your children will I give this land.' He will send his angel before you, and you shall choose a wife for my son there. And if the woman will not willingly follow you, then you shall be freed from the oath. Only do not take my son there."

So the servant gave his hand to Abraham, his master, and swore to him concerning this.

Then the servant took ten of his master's camels (for all the goods of his master were in his hands) and departed. He went up to Mesopotamia, to the city of Nahor.

There he made his camels kneel down outside the city, beside a well of water, at the time of the evening when the women go out to draw water.

Then he prayed, "O Lord God of my master Abraham, I pray you, send me good fortune today, and show kindness to my master, Abraham. You see, I stand here by the well of water, and the daughters of the men of the city come out to draw water. To one girl I shall say, 'Let down your pitcher, I beg of you, that I may drink.' If she is the wife whom you have chosen for your servant Isaac, let her say, 'Drink, and I will give your camels a drink also.' By this I shall know that you have shown kindness to my master."

It came to pass, before he had finished speaking, that Rebekah, whose father was the son of Nahor, Abraham's brother, came out with her pitcher upon her shoulder. The girl was very fair to look upon, young and unmarried. She went down to the well, filled her pitcher, and came up.

Abraham's servant ran to meet her and said, "Let me, please, drink a little water from your pitcher."

And she said, "Drink, my lord," and quickly she lowered her pitcher upon her hand and gave him a drink. When she had finished giving him a drink, she said, "I will draw water for your camels, too, until they have finished drinking."

She hurried and emptied her pitcher into the trough, and ran again to the well to draw water, and drew it for all his camels.

The man held his peace, wondering whether the Lord had made his journey successful or not. Then, as the camels finished drinking, he took out a golden earring of half a shekel weight and two bracelets for her hands, also of heavy gold.

"Whose daughter are you?" he asked. "Tell me, I beg of you, is there room in your father's house for me to spend the night there?"

She said to him, "I am the daughter of Bethuel, the son of Nahor. We have both straw and food enough, and room to lodge in."

Then the man bowed down his head and worshiped the Lord, saying, "Blessed be the Lord God of my master Abraham, who has not kept his mercy and his truth from my master, for, I being on the way, the Lord led me to the house of my master's brother."

The girl ran on to her mother's house and told these things.

Now Rebekah had a brother, and his name was Laban. When he saw the earring and the bracelets upon his sister's hands, and when he heard the words of Rebekah his sister, Laban ran out and found the servant of Abraham standing by the camels at the well.

Laban said, "Come in, you whom the Lord has blessed. Why do you stand outside? For I have prepared the house, and room for the camels."

The man came into the house, and Laban unharnessed his camels and gave them straw and feed; and he brought water to wash the man's feet and the feet of the men who were with him.

They set meat before the man to eat, but he

said, "I will not eat until I have told my errand."

So Laban said, "Speak on."

The man began, "I am Abraham's servant. The Lord has blessed my master greatly, and he has become great. The Lord has given him flocks and herds, silver and gold, menservants and maidservants, and camels and asses. And Sarah, my master's wife, bore a son to my master when she was old, and to him he has given all that he has."

Then the servant told how Abraham had sent him to find a wife for Isaac, and how the Lord had led him to Rebekah.

"And now if you will deal kindly and truly with my master, tell me, and if not, tell me, so that I may know which way to turn."

Then Laban and Bethuel answered and said, "The thing has been planned by the Lord. We cannot say anything to you, bad or good. Behold, Rebekah is here before you; take her and go, and let her be your master's son's wife, as the Lord has said."

When Abraham's servant heard their words, he worshiped the Lord, bowing himself to the earth. And he brought out jewels of silver and jewels of gold, and clothing, and gave them to Rebekah. To her brother and her mother also he gave precious things.

Then they ate and drank, he and the men that were with him, and they stayed all night. When they rose up in the morning, he said, "Send me back now to my master."

Rebekah's brother and her mother said, "Let the girl remain with us a few days, at least ten. After that she shall go with you."

But he said to them, "Do not hinder me, seeing the Lord has made my errand successful. Send me away, that I may go to my master."

"We will call the girl and ask her," they said. They called Rebekah and said to her, "Will you go with this man?"

And she said, "I will go."

So they sent away Rebekah their sister, and her nurse, and Abraham's servant, and his men. They blessed Rebekah, and Rebekah arose with her maidens, and they rode upon the camels and followed the man. And the servant took Rebekah and went his way.

JACOB AND ESAU AND THE BIRTHRIGHT

LATER when Isaac was three score years old, Rebekah bore him twin sons. The firstborn they called Esau, and the other Jacob.

The boys grew and Esau was a cunning hunter, a man of the out-of-doors, but Jacob was a plain man, dwelling in tents. Isaac loved Esau, because he liked to eat his venison, but Rebekah loved Jacob.

One day Jacob had boiled a thick soup, and Esau came from the field, and he was faint with hunger.

"Feed me, I pray you, some of that good red soup," said Esau to Jacob, "for I am faint."

"Sell me this very day your birthright," said Jacob. For Esau, being the elder, was to inherit their father's goods.

"You can see," said Esau, "I am at the point of death. What good then will this birthright do me?"

But Jacob said, "Swear to me this day."

So Esau swore to him, and he sold his birth-

right to Jacob. Then Jacob gave Esau bread and the lentil soup; and he ate and drank and rose up and went his way.

Thus Esau threw away his birthright.

23

JACOB TRICKS HIS FATHER

IT CAME to pass that when Isaac was old, and his eyes were dim, so that he could not see, he called Esau, his elder son, and said to him, "My son." And Esau said, "See, here I am."

Isaac said, "Look now, I am old, I do not know when I may die. Now therefore take your weapons, I pray you, your quiver and your bow, and go out to the field and get me some venison. Make me savory meat, such as I love, and bring it to me that I may eat, so that my soul may bless you before I die."

Now Rebekah heard when Isaac spoke to Esau his son. And Esau went to the field to hunt for venison and to bring it home.

Then Rebekah spoke to Jacob her son, saying, "Behold, I heard your father speak to Esau your brother, saying, 'Bring me venison and make me savory meat, that I may eat, and bless you before the Lord, before my death.' Now, therefore, my son, obey my voice and do as I command you.

"Go now to the flock and fetch me from it two good kids of the goats, and I will make them into savory meat for your father, such as he loves. And you shall take it to your father, that he may eat, and that he may bless you before his death."

Jacob said to Rebekah his mother, "Behold, Esau my brother is a hairy man, and I am a smooth man. Perhaps my father will feel me, and I shall seem to him a deceiver, and I shall bring a curse upon myself, and not a blessing."

But his mother said to him, "That curse would be upon me, my son. Only obey my voice and go fetch the kids to me."

So he went and fetched them to his mother; and his mother made savory meat, such as his father loved.

And Rebekah took good robes of her elder son Esau, which were in the house, and put them upon Jacob, her younger son. And she put the skins of the kids of the goats upon his hands and upon the smooth of his neck.

Then she put the savory meat, and the bread which she had prepared, into the hands of her son Jacob.

Jacob came to Isaac and said, "My father."

And Isaac said, "Here I am. Who are you, my son?"

"I am Esau, your firstborn," Jacob said to his father. "I have done as you told me. Arise, I beg of you; sit up and eat of my venison, so that your soul may bless me."

But Isaac said to his son, "How have you found it so quickly, my son?"

"Because the Lord your God brought it to me," said Jacob.

Still Isaac said to Jacob, "Come near, I beg of you, so that I may feel you, my son, whether you are really my son Esau or not."

Jacob went near to Isaac his father, and Isaac felt him and said, "The voice is Jacob's voice, but the hands are the hands of Esau." He did not recognize him, because his hands were hairy like his brother Esau's hands, so he blessed him.

Once more he said, "Are you really my son Esau?"

And Jacob said, "I am."

Then Isaac said, "Bring it near to me, and I will eat of my son's venison, that my soul may bless you."

Jacob brought the food close to him, and he ate; he brought him wine, and he drank.

Then his father Isaac said to him, "Come near now, and kiss me, my son."

And Jacob came near and kissed him, and Isaac smelled the smell of his robe and blessed him, saying:

"See, the smell of my son is as the smell of a field which the Lord has blessed. Therefore God give you of the dew of heaven and the riches of the earth, and plenty of corn and wine.

"Let people serve you, and nations bow down to you. Be lord over your brothers, and let your mother's sons bow down to you. May every one who wishes you evil be cursed, and may every one who wishes you well be blessed."

Now it happened, as soon as Isaac had finished blessing Jacob, and when Jacob had scarcely left Isaac his father, that Esau his brother came in from his hunting. And he also made savory meat and brought it to his father and said, "My father, please rise up and eat of your son's venison, so that your soul may bless me."

Then Isaac his father said to him, "Who are you?"

And he said, "I am your son, your firstborn, Esau."

Then Isaac trembled all over and said, "Who? Where is he who prepared venison and brought it to me, and I ate it before you came and have blessed him? Yes, and he shall be blessed."

When Esau heard the words of his father, he cried out a great and bitter cry, and said to his father, "Bless me, even me also, O my father!"

But Isaac said, "Your brother came with trickery and has taken away your blessing."

Esau said, "Is he not rightly named Jacob? For he has taken my place now two times. He took away my birthright, and, behold, now he has taken away my blessing." And he said, "Have you not saved a blessing for me?"

Isaac answered and said to Esau, "Behold, I have made him lord over you, and all his brothers I have given to him for servants. I have provided him with corn and wine; and what shall I do now for you, my son?"

But Esau said to his father, "Have you only one blessing, my father? Bless me, even me also, O my father!" And Esau lifted up his voice and wept.

Then Isaac his father answered and said to him, "Behold, your dwelling shall be the richness of the earth and the dews of heaven above. You shall live by the sword and shall serve your brother, but the day will come when you will have power, and you will break his yoke from off your neck."

Still Esau hated Jacob because of the blessing with which his father had blessed him; and Esau said in his heart, "When the days of mourning for my father are over, I will kill my brother Jacob."

These words of Esau her elder son were told to Rebekah. She called Jacob her younger son to her. "Watch your brother Esau," she said to him. "He comforts himself concerning you by planning to kill you.

"Now, therefore, my son, obey my voice. Arise and go to Laban my brother, at Haran. Stay with him a few days, until your brother's fury turns away, until your brother's anger turns away from you and he forgets what you have done to him. Then I will send and fetch you home again."

JACOB'S DREAM IN THE DESERT

JACOB set out from Beersheba and he started toward Haran. He came to a certain place and had to stay there all night, because the sun had set. He took some stones from the ground and he placed them for his pillow, and lay down to sleep.

Jacob dreamed, and he saw a ladder set up on the earth, the top of which reached to heaven. And he saw angels of God going up and down on it.

The Lord stood above the ladder and said to him, "I am the Lord God of Abraham, and the God of Isaac. The land on which you lie I will give to you and your children. And your children shall be as the dust of the earth; you will spread abroad to the west and to the east, to the north and to the south, and through you and your children all the families of the earth will be blessed.

"And, behold, I am with you, and I will guard you everywhere you go, and will bring you again to this place. For I will not leave you until I have done everything I have promised."

Then Jacob waked out of his sleep, and he said, "Surely the Lord is in this place, and I did not know it." He was afraid and said, "How

awesome this place is! This is surely the House of God, and this is the gate of heaven."

Early in the morning Jacob rose up and took the stone that he had used for his pillow and set it up for a pillar. Then he poured oil upon the top of it, and he called the name of that place Bethel. And Jacob vowed a vow, saying, "If God will be with me, and will guard me in the way that I go, and will give me bread to eat and clothes to wear, so that I may return again to my father's house in peace, then the Lord will be my God. And this stone, which I have set up for a pillar, will be God's house, and of all that you give to me, O God, I will give a tenth to you."

JACOB AND RACHEL

ONTINUING on his journey, Jacob came into the land of the people of the east. He looked about and saw a well in the field and three flocks of sheep lying by it, for out of that well all the flocks round about were watered.

Jacob said to the shepherds, "My brothers, where are you from?"

They replied, "We are from Haran."

"Do you know Laban, the son of Nahor?" he asked them.

And they said, "We know him."

"Is he well?" Jacob asked.

"He is well," replied the shepherds, "and see there, Rachel his daughter is coming with the sheep."

While they were still talking, Rachel came with her father's sheep, for she looked after them. When Jacob saw Rachel, the daughter of Laban, his mother's brother, and Laban's sheep, he rolled away the stone which covered the well's mouth and watered the flock. Then Jacob kissed Rachel and lifted up his voice and wept.

When Jacob told Rachel that he was her father's kin, and Rebekah's son, she ran and told her father, Laban. He hastened out to meet Jacob, and embraced him and kissed him, and brought him to his house.

Jacob told Laban all the things that had happened to him, and Laban said to him, "Surely you are my bone and flesh."

Jacob stayed with him for a month. Then Laban said to him, "Because you are my kin, should you work for me for nothing? Tell me, what shall your wages be?"

Now Laban had two daughters. The name of the elder was Leah, and the name of the younger was Rachel. Leah was tender-eyed, but Rachel was beautiful and pleasing to look upon. Jacob loved Rachel, so he said, "I will work for you seven years for Rachel, your younger daughter."

Then Laban said, "It is better for me to give her to you than to any other man; stay with me."

So Jacob worked seven years for Rachel, and they seemed to him but a few days, because he loved her.

*A*FTER *many years with Laban, Jacob had prospered exceedingly. He had much cattle, and maidservants and menservants, and camels and asses. And it came to pass that Jacob said to Laban, "Send me away, so that I may go to a place of my own, and to my own country. Give me my wife and my children, for whom I have served you, and let me go."*

Laban did not like to have Jacob leave, but at last he made a covenant with Jacob and said, "The Lord watch between me and thee, when we are absent one from the other."

Then Jacob went on his way, and the angels of the Lord met him. Jacob wrestled by night with an angel of the Lord, and at daybreak the angel said, "Your name shall no longer be called Jacob, but Israel, for you have the power of a prince with God."

And ever after, Jacob's children and his children's children were called "the children of Israel."

When Jacob heard that Esau his brother was coming to meet him with four hundred men, he was frightened, thinking that Esau still wanted to kill him. But when Esau came near, he ran to meet Jacob, and embraced him and kissed him, and they wept.

So Jacob came home to his own country.

JOSEPH IS SOLD INTO SLAVERY

OW Canaan, the land in which his father had been a stranger, became home to Jacob.

Joseph, his son, being seventeen years old, daily fed the flocks with all his brothers, the sons of his father's wives. And Joseph brought his father an evil report of them.

Now Jacob loved Joseph more than all his other children, because he was the son of his old age, so he made him a coat of many colors.

When his brothers saw that their father loved Joseph more than all his brothers, they hated Joseph and could not speak peaceably to him.

Once Joseph dreamed a dream, and he told it to his brothers, and they hated him still more. He said to them:

"Hear, I pray you, this dream which I have dreamed. We were all binding sheaves in the field, and lo, my sheaf arose and stood upright, and your sheaves stood round about and bowed down to my sheaf."

Then his brothers said to him, "Shall you indeed be king over us? Shall you really rule over us?" And they hated him still more for his dreams, and for his words.

He dreamed another dream, and told it to his brothers, saying, "Behold, I have dreamed another dream, and the sun, and the moon, and the eleven stars bowed down to me."

He told it to his father and to his brothers, and his father rebuked him, saying, "What is this dream you have dreamed? Shall your mother and I and your brothers really come to bow ourselves down to the earth before you?"

His brothers envied him, but his father remembered the words.

Now his brothers went to feed their father's flock in Shechem. One day Jacob said to Joseph, "Are your brothers not feeding the flock in Shechem? Come, I will send you to them."

"Here I am," said Joseph.

"Go, then," said Jacob, "and see whether all is well with your brothers and the flocks, and bring me word."

So he sent Joseph out of the valley of Hebron, and the boy arrived at Shechem. There a man found him wandering in the field, and the man asked him, "What are you looking for?"

"I am looking for my brothers," he said. "Can you tell me where they are feeding the flocks?"

And the man said, "They went on from here. I heard them say, 'Let us go to Dothan.'" So Joseph went on after his brothers and found them in Dothan.

When they saw him far off, even before he came close to them, they plotted against him, to slay him.

"Behold, here comes this Dreamer!" they said to one another. "Let us kill him for that and throw him into some pit. We can say some evil beast has devoured him, and then we shall see what becomes of his dreams!"

But Reuben heard this, and he said, "Let us not kill him. Shed no blood, but throw him into this pit here in the wilderness, and do not lay hands on him." He planned to save Joseph from their hands and to take him to his father again.

So it happened that when Joseph came up to his brothers, they stripped his coat from him, his coat of many colors which he was wearing, and they took him and threw him into a pit. It was an empty pit, with no water in it.

Then they sat down to eat bread; but when they lifted up their eyes and looked, there they saw a company of Ishmaelites coming from Gilead, with camels loaded with spicery and balm and myrrh, which they were carrying down to Egypt.

Then Judah said to his brothers, "What will we gain if we kill our brother and hide the deed? Come, let us sell him to the Ishmaelites, and let us not touch him, for he is our brother and our flesh."

This satisfied the brothers.

So they lifted Joseph up out of the pit and sold him to the Ishmaelites for twenty pieces of silver; and the merchants took him to Egypt.

Reuben was sad. He said to his brothers: "The child is not here, and I, where shall I go?"

But the brothers took Joseph's coat, and killed a young goat and dipped the coat in the blood. Then they took the coat of many colors and brought it to their father, and said, "We found this. Do you know whether or not it is your son's coat?"

He recognized it and said, "It is my son's coat. An evil beast has eaten him. Joseph is without doubt torn in pieces!"

Then Jacob tore his clothes and put on sackcloth, and mourned for his son many days. All his sons and all his daughters tried to comfort him, but he refused to be comforted. "I will go down to the grave," he said, "mourning for my son."

JOSEPH IN THE LAND OF EGYPT

DOWN into Egypt Joseph was brought, and Potiphar, who was an officer of Pharaoh and captain of the guard, bought him from the Ishmaelites. The Lord was with Joseph, and he became a favored servant, living in the house of his master the Egyptian. His master saw that the Lord was with him, and that the Lord made all that he did prosper in his hands. So the master approved of Joseph, and he made him overseer in his house.

The Lord blessed the Egyptian's house for Joseph's sake. So Potiphar left all that he had in Joseph's hands, and he did not even know what he owned, except the bread he ate.

Now Joseph was a handsome young man. It happened, after a while, that his master's wife loved Joseph, and when he would not love her she told her husband lies about him, and her husband was angry.

Joseph's master put him into prison where the king's prisoners were kept, and there he stayed.

But the Lord was with Joseph and showed him mercy, and made the keeper of the prison think well of him. So the keeper of the prison put all the prisoners that were in the prison into Joseph's hands, and he was in charge of them.

The keeper of the prison paid no attention to anything that went on, because the Lord was with Joseph, and whatever he did, the Lord made it prosper.

It happened, some time later, that the butler of the king of Egypt and his baker offended their lord Pharaoh, and he put them in the same prison where Joseph was kept.

three days Pharaoh will restore you to your place, and you will put Pharaoh's cup into his hands, as you used to when you were his butler.

"Only think of me when it is going well with you, and be kind to me, I beg of you, and mention me to Pharaoh, and get me out of this place. For I was really stolen away from the land of the Hebrews, and I have done nothing here that makes me deserve this dungeon."

When the chief baker saw that the interpretation was good, he said to Joseph, "I also had a dream, and in it I had three white baskets on my head. In the topmost basket were all kinds of baked goods for Pharaoh, and the birds ate them out of the basket upon my head."

Joseph answered him and said, "This is the meaning of it: The three baskets are three days. Within three days Pharaoh will call you up and hang you on a tree, and the birds will eat your flesh."

It happened that on the third day, which was Pharaoh's birthday, he made a feast for all his servants, and he called up the chief butler and

The captain of the guard turned them over to Joseph and he looked after them, and they stayed on in prison for some time.

Now one night each of them dreamed a dream, and each of them a different dream, the butler and the baker of the king of Egypt. And when Joseph came in to them in the morning and looked at them, he saw that they were sad. He asked, "Why do you look so sad today?"

"We have dreamed a dream," they said to him, "and there is no one to interpret it for us."

Joseph said, "Do not interpretations come from God? Tell me the dreams."

So the chief butler told his dream to Joseph, saying, "In my dream I saw a vine before me, and on the vine were three branches. It seemed as though it budded and the blossoms shot forth, and the clusters grew into ripe grapes. Pharaoh's cup was in my hand, and I took the grapes and pressed them into Pharaoh's cup, and I put the cup into Pharaoh's hand."

Joseph said to him, "This is the interpretation of it: The three branches are three days. Within

the chief baker among his servants. He returned the chief butler to his butlership again, and the butler gave the cup to Pharaoh; but Pharaoh hanged the chief baker, as Joseph had said.

Yet the chief butler did not remember Joseph, but forgot him.

Two whole years went by, and then it happened one night that Pharaoh dreamed. He stood by the river, and there came up out of the river seven handsome, fat cows, and they fed in a meadow. Then seven other cows came up after them out of the river, scrawny and thin, and stood by the other cows upon the brink of the river. And the scrawny and thin cows ate up the seven fat and handsome cows. Then Pharaoh awoke.

He slept again and dreamed the second time. He saw seven ears of corn come up on one stalk, hardy and good. Then seven thin ears, blasted by the east wind, sprang up after them, and the seven thin ears devoured the seven hardy and full ears.

Pharaoh awoke and knew it was a dream, but

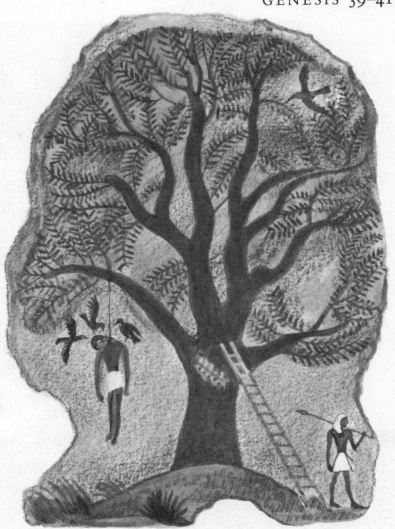

in the morning his spirit was troubled. He sent for all the magicians of Egypt, and all the wise men of the land. Pharaoh told them his dream, but there was no one who could interpret them to Pharaoh.

Then the chief butler spoke to Pharaoh and said, "Today I remember my faults. Pharaoh was angry with his servants and put the chief baker and me in the prison of the captain of the guard. We each dreamed a dream one night, he and I, and there was in prison with us a young man, a Hebrew, servant to the captain of the guard. We told him our dreams, and he interpreted them to us; to each man he gave the meaning of his dream. And everything happened just as he told us; I was restored to my office, and the baker was hanged."

Then Pharaoh sent for Joseph, and they brought him hastily out of the dungeon. He shaved himself and changed his clothing and came in to Pharaoh.

Pharaoh said to Joseph, "I have dreamed a dream, and no one can interpret it. I have heard

33

it said that you can understand a dream and tell its meaning."

Joseph answered Pharaoh, saying, "It is not my power. God shall give Pharaoh an answer."

Then Pharaoh told Joseph his dreams, and Joseph said to Pharaoh, "The two dreams of Pharaoh are one. God has shown Pharaoh what he is about to do.

"The seven good cows are seven years, and the seven good ears are seven years; the dream is the same. The seven thin and scrawny cows that came up after them are seven years, and the seven empty ears, blasted with the east wind, will be seven years of famine. What God is about to do he is showing Pharaoh.

"There will be seven years of great plenty throughout the whole land of Egypt. And after them will come seven years of famine, and all the plenty will be forgotten in the land of Egypt, and the famine will consume the land.

"For this reason the dream was sent to Pharaoh twice; the thing has been planned by God, and he will make it happen soon.

"Now, therefore, let Pharaoh search for a man discreet and wise, and set him over the land of Egypt. Let Pharaoh do this, and let him appoint officers to control the land, and gather up a fifth of the harvest of the land of Egypt in the seven years of plenty.

"Let them gather up the food of those good years that come, and store up grain under the order of Pharaoh, and let them keep food in the cities. And that food shall be for the land to draw on during the seven years of famine, which shall come in the land of Egypt, so that the land may not perish through the famine."

This plan seemed good to Pharaoh, and to all his advisers. But Pharaoh said to his servants, "Can we find such a man as this, a man in whom the spirit of God is?"

Then Pharaoh said to Joseph, "Inasmuch as God has shown you all this, there is no one as discreet and wise as you. You shall be in charge of my house, and according to your word all my people will be ruled. Only on the throne itself will I be greater than you." And he said, "See, I have set you over all the land of Egypt."

Then Pharaoh took off his ring from his hand and put it upon Joseph's hand, and dressed him in robes of fine linen and put a gold chain about his neck. And he made him ride in the second royal chariot, and people cried before him, "Bow the knee!" So Pharaoh made him ruler over all the land of Egypt.

Then Pharaoh gave Joseph an Egyptian name, and an Egyptian wife, and Joseph was known throughout all the land of Egypt. Joseph was then thirty years old.

Joseph traveled all over the land of Egypt. In the seven years of plenty the earth yielded grain in abundance. And Joseph gathered up food in those seven years in the land of Egypt, and stored up the food in the cities; in each city he stored the harvest of the fields which were around it.

Joseph gathered grain as the sand of the sea, so much that he stopped counting, for it was without number.

Two sons were born to Joseph before the years of famine came, and he called the firstborn Manasseh, and the second Ephraim.

Then the seven years of plenty in the land of Egypt were ended, and the seven years of poverty began, just as Joseph had said. The famine was in all countries, but in the land of Egypt there was food.

When all the land of Egypt was hungry, the people cried to Pharaoh for bread, and Pharaoh said to all the Egyptians, "Go to Joseph, and do as he tells you."

As the famine spread over the face of the earth, Joseph opened all the storehouses and sold food to the Egyptians, for the famine was severe in Egypt, too. And from all countries people came to Egypt to Joseph to buy grain, because the famine was so severe in all lands.

JOSEPH'S BROTHERS IN EGYPT

AS soon as Jacob heard that there was grain in Egypt, he said to his sons, "Why do you sit and look at one another? I have heard that in Egypt there is grain. Go down and buy some for us there, so that we may live and not die."

So Joseph's ten brothers set out to buy grain in Egypt. Benjamin, Joseph's youngest brother, did not go with them. "For harm might befall him," said Jacob.

So, among the crowds that came to buy grain, came the sons of Jacob, for the famine was in the land of Canaan, too.

Now Joseph was the governor of the land, and it was he who sold to all the people of the land, and Joseph's brothers came and bowed themselves before him with their faces to the earth.

When Joseph saw his brothers, he recognized them, but he acted like a stranger toward them, and he spoke roughly to them.

"Where did you come from?" he said.

"From the land of Canaan to buy food," they answered.

Joseph's brothers did not know him. He remembered the dreams he had dreamed of them, and he said to them, "You are spies; you have come to see the nakedness of the land."

"We are twelve brothers," they said, "the sons of one man in the land of Canaan. The youngest one is with our father now, and one is no more."

But Joseph said again, "It is just as I told you: you are spies. This shall be the proof; by the life of Pharaoh, you shall not go out of here unless your youngest brother comes to this place. Send one of you and let him fetch your brother, and you shall be kept in prison so that it may be proved whether there is any truth in your words. Otherwise, by the life of Pharaoh, surely you are spies!"

And he put them all under guard for three days.

The third day Joseph said to them, "Do this and save your lives, for I am a God-fearing man. If you are honest men, let one of your brothers stay bound in prison. The rest of you take grain to feed the hungry in your houses. But bring your youngest brother to me; this will prove your words are true, and you shall not die."

They decided to do this, saying to one another, "Truly we are guilty about our brother, for we saw the suffering of his soul, when he pleaded with us, and we would not listen; that is why this distress has come to us."

And Reuben answered them, saying, "Did I not speak to you, saying, 'Do not sin against the child,' and you would not listen? Because

of that we must settle now for his blood."

Now they did not know that Joseph understood them, for he spoke to them through an interpreter, but he turned away from them and wept. Turning back again, he spoke to them and took Simeon from them and bound him before their eyes.

Then Joseph commanded servants to fill their sacks with grain, and to put every man's money back into his sack, and to give them provisions for the journey. That was how he treated them.

They loaded their asses with the corn, and started home.

When one of them opened his sack to feed his ass at an inn where they stopped, he spied his money, for it was in the mouth of his sack. And the others also found money in their sacks. Then their hearts failed them and they were afraid, and said to one another, "What is this that God has done to us?"

They came home to Jacob their father in the land of Canaan and told him all that had happened to them.

Jacob said to them, "You have taken away my children from me. Joseph is no more, and Simeon is no more, and you want to take Benjamin away. All these things are hard."

Then Reuben spoke to his father, saying, "You may kill my two sons if I do not bring Benjamin back to you. Put him into my hands, and I will bring him to you again."

But Jacob said, "My son shall not go down with you, for his brother is dead, and he alone is left. If harm should come to him on the journey, you would bring down my gray hairs with sorrow to the grave."

BENJAMIN GOES TO EGYPT

HE FAMINE continued in the land. And the time came when Jacob and his sons had eaten up the grain which the sons had brought up from Egypt, and their father said to them, "Go again, buy us some food."

But Judah told him, "If you will send our brother with us, we will go down and buy you food, but if you will not send him, we will not go down, for the man said to us, 'You shall not see my face unless your brother is with you.'"

"Why did you deal so badly with me as to tell the man you had another brother?" asked Jacob.

And they explained, "The man asked us strictly about ourselves and our family, saying, 'Is your father still alive? Have you another brother?' And we answered his questions. How could we know that he would say, 'Bring your brother down'?"

Judah said to his father Jacob, "Send the lad with me, and we shall get up and go, so that we may live and not die, we and you yourself, and all our little ones.

"I will be responsible for him, and you may

demand him of me. If I do not bring him to you and set him before you, then let me bear the blame forever. If we had not lingered so long, surely we would already have been back a second time."

Then their father said to them, "If it must be so now, do this: take some of the best fruits of the land in your containers, and carry down to the man a present, a little balm, and a little honey, spices, and myrrh, nuts and almonds. Carry double money with you, and take back again the money that you brought home in the mouths of your sacks, for perhaps it was an oversight.

"Take your brother, too, and go again to the man. May God Almighty grant you mercy from the man, so that he may send home

Simeon and Benjamin. For if I must grieve for my children, it is bitter grief indeed."

And the men took presents, and double money and Benjamin, and started off and went down to Egypt, and came before Joseph.

When Joseph saw Benjamin with them, he said to the manager of his house, "Take these men home, and kill some meat, and make it ready, for these men will dine with me at noon."

The servant did as Joseph told him, and brought the brothers to Joseph's house. But the men were afraid because they were taken to Joseph's house, and they said, "Because of the money that was returned in our sacks the first time we are being brought in here, so that he may find some fault with us, and fall upon us, and take us for slaves, and seize our asses, too."

So they approached the steward of Joseph's house, and they spoke to him at the doorway.

"O sir," they said, "we came down the first time just to buy food, but it happened that when we came to the inn and opened our sacks, behold, every man's money was in the mouth of his sack, our money in full amount, so we have brought it back with us.

"We have brought other money down, too, to buy food. We do not know who put the money in our sacks."

"Peace be to you!" said the steward. "Fear not. Your God, the God of your father, gave you the treasure in your sacks. I had your money."

Then he brought Simeon out to them.

The man took the brothers into Joseph's house and gave them water, and they washed their feet, and he gave their asses food. Meanwhile they prepared the present to give to Joseph when he came in at noon, for they had been told that they were to eat there.

When Joseph came home, they gave him the present which they had brought into the house, and they bowed themselves down to the earth before him.

He asked them how they were and said, "Is your father well, the old man of whom you spoke? Is he still alive?"

"Your servant our father is in good health," they answered. "He is still alive." And they bowed down their heads respectfully.

Lifting up his eyes, Joseph saw his brother Benjamin, his own mother's son, and he said, "Is this your younger brother, of whom you told me?" And he added, "God be gracious to you, my son."

Then Joseph hurried away, for his heart yearned for his brother, and he sought a place to weep. He went into his room and wept there. Then he washed his face and calmed himself and went out and said, "Serve the food."

The servants served him separately, and themselves separately, and Joseph's brothers also by themselves. The Egyptians could not eat a meal with the Hebrews, for that was against their laws.

The brothers sat before Joseph in order, from the firstborn with his birthright down to the youngest in his youth, and the men marveled at one another.

Joseph sent servings to them from his table, but Benjamin's serving was five times as much as any of the others. And they drank and were merry with him.

He gave orders to the steward of his house, saying, "Fill the men's sacks with food, as much as they can carry, and put every man's money in his sack's mouth. And put my cup, the silver cup, in the sack's mouth of the youngest with his grain money."

The steward did everything just as Joseph told him.

As soon as the morning was light, the men were sent away, they and their asses. And when they had left the city, but were not yet far off, Joseph said to his steward, "Up, follow the men! And when you have overtaken them, say to them, 'Why have you returned evil for good? That was the cup from which my lord drank, and which he used in making prophecies. You have done evil!'"

The steward set out at once and overtook the brothers. He spoke to them in the very same words. But they said to him, "Why does my lord say these things? God forbid that your servants should do anything like this. Look, the money which we found in our sacks' mouths we brought back to you from the land of Canaan; would we then steal silver or gold out of your lord's house?

"Let whoever is found to have it die, and the rest of us will be your lord's slaves."

He said, "Now let it be just as you say, but he who is found to have it shall be my servant, and the rest of you shall go free."

Then each man speedily put down his sack on the ground, and each man opened his sack. The steward searched, beginning with the eldest and finishing with the youngest, and the cup was found in Benjamin's sack.

Then Joseph's brothers tore their clothes, and each man loaded his ass, and they returned to the city. When they came to Joseph's house, they fell down before him on the ground.

Joseph said to them, "What is this that you have done? Do you not know that a man like me can see through these things?"

And Judah said, "What shall we say to my lord? How shall we speak? Or how shall we clear ourselves? God has found out the wickedness of your servants. Behold, we are my lord's servants, all of us as well as he in whose sack the cup was found."

"God forbid that I should demand that," he said, "but the man in whose hand the cup was found, he shall be my servant. As for the rest of you, go in peace up to your father."

Then Judah came closer to him and said, "Oh, my lord, let your servant, I beg of you, speak a word in my lord's ear, and do not let your anger burn against your servant, for you are as powerful as Pharaoh.

"My lord asked his servants, 'Have you a father or a brother?' And we said, 'We have a father, an old man, and a child of his old age, a little boy, whose brother is dead and he alone is left of his mother, and his father loves him.'

"And you said to your servants, 'Bring him down to me, that I may have a look at him.' And we said to my lord, 'The lad cannot leave his father, for if he should leave his father, his father would die.' And you said, 'Unless your youngest brother comes down with you, you will not see my face again.'

"So when we came up to your servant our father, we told him your words. When our father said, 'Go again, and buy us a little food,' we said, 'We cannot go down; only if our youngest brother is with us can we go, for we may not see the man's face unless our youngest brother is with us.'

"And your servant our father said to us, 'You know that my wife bore me two sons, and the one I lost and surely he is torn to pieces and I have not seen him since; and if you take this one from me, too, and any harm befalls him, you will bring down my gray hairs with sorrow to the grave.'

"Now, therefore, when I come to your servant our father and the lad is not with us,

seeing that his life is bound up with the lad's life, he shall surely die; and your servants will have brought down their father to the grave with sorrow.

"For your servant took responsibility for the lad to my father, saying, 'If I do not bring him back to you, then I shall bear the blame forever.'

"Now, therefore, I beg of you, let your servant stay instead of the lad, a slave to my lord, and let the lad go home with his brothers. For how can I go home to my father if the lad

is not with me, and see the evil that would come to my father?"

Then Joseph could not control himself before the Egyptians around him, and he cried, "Let everyone leave me!" So the Egyptians departed, and Joseph made himself known to his brothers. But he wept aloud, and the Egyptians and Pharaoh's household heard it.

Joseph said to his brothers, "I am Joseph. Is my father still alive?"

And his brothers could not answer him, for

they were all overcome with wonderment.

Then Joseph said to his brothers, "Come close to me, I beg you." They came near, and he said, "I am Joseph, your brother, whom you sold into Egypt. Now do not grieve nor be angry with yourselves because you sold me here, for God sent me here ahead of you, to save your lives.

"For two years now the famine has been in the land, and there are five years to come in which there shall be neither tilling nor harvest. God sent me before you to preserve your families on the earth and to save your lives. So it was not really you that sent me here, but God; and he has made me an adviser to Pharaoh, and

lord of his household, and a ruler throughout the land of Egypt.

"Hurry now, and go up to my father and say to him, 'Your son Joseph says, "God has made me lord of all Egypt; come down to me without delay. You shall dwell in the land of Goshen, and you shall be near me, you and your children and your children's children, and your flocks and your herds, and all you own. And I will nourish you here, for there are still five years of famine to come and you and your household would otherwise know poverty."'

"Now your eyes and Benjamin's can see that it is really I who speak to you. And you are to tell my father of all my honors in Egypt, and of

43

all you have seen. Go and hurry, and bring my father down here."

Then he embraced Benjamin and wept, and Benjamin wept.

He kissed all his brothers, and wept with them, and after that his brothers talked with him.

News of the reunion was heard in Pharaoh's house. "Joseph's brothers have come," it was said. And Pharaoh and his servants were pleased.

Pharaoh said to Joseph, "Say to your brothers, 'Load your beasts, and go, hurry up to the land of Canaan. Get your father and your households and come to me, and I will give you the best of the land of Egypt, and you shall eat of the fat of the land. These are your orders: Take wagons up from Egypt for your little ones and your wives, and bring your father and come back. Do not bring with you your goods, for the best of all the land of Egypt shall be yours.'"

Therefore Joseph gave his brothers wagons, and gave them provisions for the journey. To each of them he gave changes of clothes, but to Benjamin he gave three hundred pieces of silver and five changes of clothes. And to his father he sent these gifts: ten asses loaded with the good things of Egypt, and ten she asses loaded with corn and bread and meat for his provisions on the journey.

So he sent his brothers away, and they left. And he said to them, "See that you do not have any trouble on the way."

They went up out of Egypt and came to the land of Canaan, to Jacob their father. They told him everything, saying, "Joseph is still alive, and he is governor over all the land of Egypt." Jacob's heart grew faint, for he could not believe it.

They told him every word Joseph had said to them, and when he saw the wagons which Joseph had sent to carry him, Jacob at last believed.

"It is enough," Jacob said. "Joseph my son is still alive. I will go and see him before I die."

MOSES IN THE BULRUSHES

OME years later Joseph died, and a new Pharaoh was king over Egypt. He said to his people, "The people of Israel are more numerous and mightier than we are. Come, let us deal wisely with them, lest they should outnumber us and, in case of war, should join our enemies and fight against us. We must get them out of the land."

Therefore the Egyptians set over the Israelites taskmasters to make them work very hard. And they built for Pharaoh treasure cities, Pithom and Rameses. But the more the Egyptians mistreated them, the more they grew in strength and increased in numbers. And the Egyptians were worried because of the children of Israel.

So Pharaoh commanded all his people with these words: "Every son that is born to the Israelites you shall cast into the river, and every daughter you shall save alive."

Now a man of the house of Levi married a daughter of the house of Levi, and the woman bore a son. When she saw that he was a sturdy

45

child, she hid him for three months and when she could not hide him any longer, she took a covered basket of bulrushes, daubed it with pitch, and laid the baby in it. Then she put it among the reeds by the river's bank. The baby's sister stood at a distance to see what would happen to him.

The daughter of Pharaoh came down to wash herself at the river, and her maids walked along by the riverside. When she saw the basket among the reeds, she sent her maid to fetch it. And she opened it, and saw the child, and the baby began to cry. She took pity on him, and said, "This is one of the Hebrews' children."

Then the baby's sister said to Pharaoh's daughter, "Shall I go and bring you a nurse of the Hebrew women, so that she may nurse the child for you?"

"Go," said Pharaoh's daughter, and the girl went and called the child's mother.

Pharaoh's daughter said to her, "Take this child away and nurse it for me, and I will give you your wages." So the woman took her own child and nursed him.

When the child grew older, she took him to Pharaoh's daughter, and he became her son. She called him Moses "Because," she said, "I drew him out of the water."

MOSES IN EXILE

T HAPPENED in those days, when Moses was grown, that he went out among his kinsmen and saw how heavily burdened they were; and he saw an Egyptian striking a Hebrew, one of his kinsmen. He looked this way and that way, and when he saw that there was no one near, he killed the Egyptian and hid him in the sand.

When he went out the next day, he saw two of the Hebrew men fighting each other, and he said to the one who was in the wrong, "Why did you strike this man?"

The man said, "Who made you a prince and a judge over us? Do you intend to kill me as you killed the Egyptian?"

Then Moses was afraid, for he thought, "Surely my misdeed is known."

When Pharaoh heard this story, he tried to kill Moses, but Moses fled from Pharaoh's presence and lived in the land of Midian.

There one day he sat down beside a well. Now the priest of Midian had seven daughters, and they came and drew water, and filled the troughs to water their father's flock. Shepherds came and drove them away, but Moses stood up and helped them and watered their flock.

When they came home to Reuel their father, he said, "How is it that you are here so early today?"

And they said, "An Egyptian defended us from the shepherds, and also drew water enough for us and watered the flocks."

"Well, where is he?" he said to his daughters. "Why did you leave the man? Ask him to come and eat with us."

Later Moses decided to live with this man, and the man gave Moses his daughter Zipporah for a wife. She bore him a son, and Moses called him Gershom, for he said, "I have been a stranger in a strange land."

MOSES AND THE BURNING BUSH

UNDER harsh masters the children of Israel sighed against their slavery, and they cried out, and their cry came up unto God. God heard their groaning and remembered his covenant with Abraham, with Isaac, and with Jacob. And God looked down upon the children of Israel, and had pity upon them.

At this time Moses was keeping the flock of Jethro (or Reuel), his father-in-law, the priest of Midian, and he led the flock to the far side of the desert and came to the mountain of God, to Horeb. And the angel of the Lord appeared to him in a flame of fire from the middle of a bush. He looked, and saw that the bush burned with fire, but it was not destroyed.

Then Moses said, "I will turn aside now and see this great sight, and learn why the bush is not burnt."

When the Lord saw that he turned aside to see, God called to him out of the middle of the bush: "Moses, Moses."

He answered, "Here am I."

"Do not come near," God said. "Take your shoes off your feet, for the place where you are standing is holy ground." And he said also, "I am the God of your father, the God of Abraham, the God of Isaac, and the God of Jacob."

Then Moses hid his face, for he was afraid to look upon God.

· The Lord said, "I have certainly seen the hardships of my people who are in Egypt, and have heard their cries because of their taskmasters. Because I know their sorrows, I have come down to deliver them from the grasp of the Egyptians and to bring them out of that land to a land good and large, a land flowing with milk and honey. Now you can see that the cry of the children of Israel has come to me, and I have also seen the hardships with which the Egyptians bow them down.

"Come now, therefore, and I will send you to Pharaoh, so that you may lead forth my people, the children of Israel, out of Egypt."

But Moses said to God, "Who am I, that I should go to Pharaoh, and that I should lead out the children of Israel from Egypt?"

The Lord said, "Certainly I will be with you, and this shall be a token to you that I have sent you: When you have led forth the people out of Egypt, you shall worship God upon this mountain."

Moreover God said to Moses, "Go and gather the elders of Israel together, and say to them, 'The Lord God of your fathers, the God of Abraham, of Isaac, and of Jacob, appeared to me,' and tell them all I have said to you."

Moses answered and said, "But they will not believe me nor listen to my voice; for they will say, 'The Lord has not appeared to you.'"

Then the Lord said to him, "What is that in your hand?"

And he said, "A rod."

"Cast it on the ground," he said. And he cast it on the ground, and it became a serpent, and Moses ran away from it.

The Lord said to Moses, "Put out your hand and take it by the tail." So he put out his hand and caught the serpent, and it became a rod in his hand. "That is so they may believe that the Lord God of their fathers, the God of Abraham, the God of Isaac, and the God of Jacob, has appeared to you."

Furthermore the Lord said to him, "Put your hand against your breast now."

He put his hand against his breast, and when he took it away, he saw that his hand was white as snow and diseased.

The Lord said, "Put your hand against your breast again," and he put his hand against his breast again, and when he took it away, behold, it had turned again like his other flesh.

"It shall come to pass, if they will not believe you nor be impressed by the first sign, that they will believe the second sign. But if they will not believe either of these two signs, nor listen to your voice, you shall take water from the river and pour it on the dry land. And the water which you take out of the river will become blood on the dry land."

Still Moses said to the Lord, "O my Lord, I am not a good speaker; I was not before, and I am not since you have spoken to your servant; but I am slow of speech, and have a slow tongue."

The Lord said to him, "Who has made man's mouth? Who makes the dumb, the deaf, the seeing, or the blind? Have not I, the Lord, done it? You go now, and I will be with your mouth and will teach you what to say."

He said, "O my Lord, send, I beg you, whom you will send."

Then the Lord became angry with Moses, and he said, "Is not Aaron the Levite your brother? I know that he can speak well. Also, I see that he is coming out to meet you, and when he sees you, he will be glad at heart. You shall

speak to him and put words in his mouth. And I will be with your mouth and with his, and will teach you what you shall do. He shall be your spokesman to the people; he shall take the place of a mouth to you, and you shall be to him like a God. Also you shall take this rod in your hand, to do signs with it."

Then Moses went home, back to his father-in-law Jethro, and said to him, "Let me go, I beg of you, and let me return to my kinfolk who are in Egypt, and see if they are still alive."

Jethro said to Moses, "Go in peace."

Then the Lord said to Moses in Midian, "Go, return to Egypt, for all the men are dead who sought your life."

So Moses took his wife and his sons, and set them upon an ass, and returned to the land of Egypt.

And the Lord said to Aaron, "Go into the wilderness to meet Moses."

And Aaron went and met Moses at the mountain of God, and kissed him. And Moses told Aaron all that the Lord had told him, and the signs he had taught him.

So Moses and Aaron gathered together all the elders of the children of Israel, and Aaron spoke all the words which the Lord had told Moses, and they did all the signs for the people to see.

Then the people believed, and when they heard that the Lord had visited the children of Israel, and that he had seen their hardships, they bowed their heads and worshiped.

THE PLAGUES OF EGYPT

OSES and Aaron went in to Pharaoh and told him, "These are the words of the Lord God of Israel: 'Let my people go, so that they may hold a feast to me in the wilderness.'" Pharaoh said, "Who is the Lord that I should obey his voice and let Israel go? I do not know the Lord; neither will I let Israel go."

The same day Pharaoh commanded the taskmasters of the people, and their officers, saying, "You shall not give the people straw to make bricks any more, as you have done. Let them go and gather straw for themselves. And the number of bricks which they made before, you are still to demand of them. You shall not lessen it at all, for they are idle. That is why they cry out, saying, 'Let us go and sacrifice to our God.'"

The taskmasters went out and told the people, "Pharaoh says, 'I will not give you straw. Go out and get straw where you can find it, but do not let your work fall behind.'"

Then the people met Moses and Aaron, who stood in the road as they came out from Pharaoh, and they said to them, "May the Lord look upon you and judge you because you have made us have a bad reputation in Pharaoh's eyes and in the eyes of his servants, so that they want to kill us."

Then Moses turned back to the Lord and said, "Lord, why have you treated these people so badly? Why have you sent me? For since I came to Pharaoh to speak in your name, he has been wicked to these people, and you have not done anything to save them."

The Lord said to Moses, "You shall say all that I will tell you, and Aaron your brother will tell it to Pharaoh, so that he may send the children of Israel out of his land. But I will harden Pharaoh's heart and perform many signs and miracles in the land of Egypt. Still Pharaoh will not listen to you, so that I may lay my hand on Egypt and bring forth my armies and my people, the children of Israel, out of Egypt by my great power. And the Egyptians shall know

that I am the Lord, when I stretch forth my hand upon Egypt and bring the children of Israel out from among them."

Moses and Aaron did whatever the Lord commanded them. Moses was eighty years old and Aaron was eighty-three years old when they spoke to Pharaoh.

The Lord spoke to Moses and to Aaron, saying, "When Pharaoh asks you to show him a miracle, then you say to Aaron, 'Take your rod and cast it before Pharaoh,' and it will become a serpent."

So Moses and Aaron went in to Pharaoh, and they did as the Lord commanded them, and Aaron cast down the rod before Pharaoh and his servants, and it became a serpent.

Then Pharaoh called all the wise men and the sorcerers and the magicians of Egypt. In the same manner each man cast down his rod, and they became serpents. But Aaron's rod swallowed up their rods.

Then the Lord hardened Pharaoh's heart, so that he did not pay any attention to them, as the Lord had said.

The Lord said to Moses, "Pharaoh's heart is hardened. He refuses to let the people go. Go to

Pharaoh again in the morning. He is going out to the river; so you stand by the river bank until he comes, and take the rod which turned to a serpent in your hand.

"You shall say to him, 'The Lord God of the Hebrews has sent me to you, saying, "Let my people go, that they may worship me in the wilderness," and still up to this time you would not listen. Now these are the words of the Lord: "In this way you shall know that I am the Lord." See, I will strike the rod that is in my hand upon the water in the river, and it shall be turned to blood. And the fish in the river will die, and the river will smell foul, and the Egyptians will not be able to drink the water of the river.'"

Then the Lord said further to Moses, "Say to Aaron, 'Take your rod and stretch out your hand upon the waters of Egypt, upon her streams, upon her rivers, and her ponds and all her pools of water, so that they may become blood, so that there may be blood throughout all the land of Egypt, in all the jars of wood and jugs of stone.'"

Moses and Aaron did all this just as the Lord commanded; Aaron lifted up the rod and struck the water in the river, in the sight of Pharaoh

and his servants, and all the water in the river was turned to blood. And the fish in the river died, and the river smelled foul, so that the Egyptians could not drink the water of the river.

But the magicians of Egypt could do that with their enchantments, so Pharaoh's heart was hardened, and he did not pay any attention to Moses and Aaron, as the Lord had said.

Then Pharaoh turned and went into his house, his heart unmoved by this. And all the Egyptians dug round about the river for water to drink, for they could not drink of the water of the river for seven days after the Lord had smitten the waters.

Then the Lord said to Moses, "Go to Pharaoh, and say to him, 'These are the words of the Lord: "Let my people go, so that they may worship me. If you refuse to let them go, then I will punish your whole country with frogs. The river will bring forth quantities of frogs, which will come into your house and into your bedroom and onto your bed, and into the houses of your servants, and upon your people, and into your ovens and into your kitchens. The frogs will swarm over you and your people and your servants."'"

Then the Lord said further to Moses, "Tell Aaron to stretch out his hand with your rod over the streams, over the rivers and the ponds, and make frogs swarm over the land of Egypt."

Aaron stretched out his hand over the waters of Egypt, and the frogs came up and covered the land.

But the magicians also could do this, and they brought up frogs over Egypt.

Pharaoh called for Moses and Aaron, and said, "Speak to your Lord and ask him to take away the frogs from me and from my people, and I will let the people go to make sacrifices to their Lord."

Then Moses said to Pharaoh, "O glorious king, when shall I ask, for you and for your servants and for your people, to have the frogs taken away from you and your houses, so that they may remain only in the river?"

He said, "Tomorrow."

And Moses said, "It shall be just as you say, so that you may know that there is no one like the Lord our God. The frogs shall be taken from you and from your houses, and from your servants and from your people. They shall remain in the river alone."

Moses and Aaron left Pharaoh, and Moses spoke to the Lord about the frogs which he had brought down upon Pharaoh. The Lord did as Moses asked: the frogs died out of the houses, out of the villages, and out of the fields. And they were gathered up in heaps, and the whole land smelled of them.

When Pharaoh saw that there was relief from them, he hardened his heart and would not listen to Moses and Aaron, just as the Lord had said.

THEN the Lord sent dust which turned to lice on all the men and beasts; he sent swarms of flies, and a plague upon the cattle, and a siege of boils and blisters upon the men; but still the Lord hardened Pharaoh's heart and he would not listen to Moses and Aaron.

The Lord sent thunder and hail, and fire ran along the ground; and the Lord rained hail upon the land of Egypt. And the hail struck down every growing thing in the fields and broke every tree of the fields. Only in the land of Goshen, where the children of Israel were, was there no hail.

But still the heart of Pharaoh was hard, and he would not let the children of Israel go.

The Lord sent a plague of locusts, and he sent a great darkness which hung over all the land of Egypt for three days, a darkness so thick that it could be felt. Each time Pharaoh promised to let the children of Israel go, but each time the Lord hardened his heart so that he would not.

Then the Lord gave Moses directions for the last and most terrible plague, and he said, "Afterward he will surely let you go."

THE NIGHT OF THE PASSOVER

THEN *Moses called for all the elders of Israel, and told them what the Lord had told him:*

CHOOSE a lamb according to the size of your families, and kill it. Take a bunch of herbs and dip it in the blood that is in the basin, and strike with the blood the top piece and the two side posts of the door of your house; and none of you shall go out the door until morning.

"For the Lord will pass through to strike the Egyptians, and when he sees the blood upon the lintel and on the two side posts, the Lord will pass over the door, and will not allow death to come into your houses to strike you.

"And you shall observe this thing as an order from God to you and your sons forever. It shall come to pass when you come to the land which the Lord will give you, according to his promise, that you shall keep this service. And when your children say, 'What do you mean by this service?' you shall say, 'It is the sacrifice of the Lord's passover, for he passed over the houses of the children of Israel in Egypt when he struck down the Egyptians, and he saved our families.'"

The people bowed their heads and worshiped. Then the children of Israel went away and did as the Lord had commanded Moses and Aaron.

And it came to pass that at midnight the Lord struck down all the firstborn in the land of Egypt, from the firstborn child of Pharaoh on his throne to the firstborn of the captive in the dungeon, and all the firstborn of cattle.

Pharaoh rose up in the night, he and all his servants, and all the Egyptians, and there was a great cry in Egypt, for there was not a house where there was not one dead.

Pharaoh called for Moses and Aaron at night, and said, "Rise up and get out from among my people, both you and all the children of Israel, and go worship your Lord, as you have been saying."

The Egyptians were urging the people, trying to send them out of the land in haste, for they said, "We are all dead men."

So the people took their dough before it was raised, and bound their kneading boards up in their clothes bundles on their shoulders. And the people of Israel departed and journeyed from Rameses to Succoth.

CROSSING THE RED SEA

ONTINUING their journey from Succoth, they camped at Etham, at the edge of the wilderness. And the Lord went before them by day in a pillar of cloud to show them the way, and by night in a pillar of fire to give them light, so they could travel by day and night. He did not take away the pillar of cloud by day nor the pillar of fire by night, from the people.

It was told to the king of Egypt that the people had fled, and the hearts of Pharaoh and his servants were turned against the people, and they said, "Why have we done this, and let Israel free from serving us?"

Then Pharaoh made ready his chariot and took his people with him. He took six hundred chosen chariots, of all the chariots of Egypt, and put captains over all of them.

The Lord hardened the heart of Pharaoh, king of Egypt, and Pharaoh pursued the children of Israel, for the children of Israel had gone out proudly.

The Egyptians came after them, all the horses

and chariots of Pharaoh, his horsemen and his army, and overtook them camping beside the sea, near Pihahiroth in front of Baalzephon.

When Pharaoh came near, the children of Israel looked up, and, seeing the Egyptians marching after them, they were badly frightened. Then the children of Israel cried out to the Lord, and they said to Moses, "Were there no graves in Egypt? Have you brought us away to die in the wilderness? Why have you treated us so, in bringing us out of Egypt? Did we not tell you in Egypt, 'Let us alone, so that we can serve the Egyptians'? For it would have been better for us to serve the Egyptians than to die in the wilderness."

"Do not be afraid," Moses said to the people. "Stand still and see the power of the Lord to save you, as he will show it to you today; for the Egyptians whom you have seen today you will never see again, forever. The Lord will fight for you, if you will have patience."

The Lord said to Moses, "Why are you crying to me? Tell the children of Israel to go forward. Just lift up your rod and stretch out your hand over the sea, and it will divide, and the children of Israel will go on dry ground through the middle of the sea.

"And you will see that I will harden the hearts of the Egyptians, and they will follow you; then I will show my power to Pharaoh

and all his host and his chariots and his horse-men. And the Egyptians will know that I am the Lord, when I have shown them my power."

Then the angel of God which went before the camp of Israel moved and went behind them; the pillar of cloud moved from in front of them and rose up behind them. It came between the camp of Israel and the camp of the Egyptians, and was a cloud of darkness to the Egyptians, but it gave light by night to Israel, so that the Egyptians did not come near Israel all night.

Then Moses stretched out his hand over the sea, and the Lord caused the sea to go back by making a strong east wind to blow all that night; it made the sea dry land, and the waters were divided.

The children of Israel walked into the middle of the sea upon the dry ground, and the waters were a wall on their right hand and on their left.

The Egyptians pursued them and went into the middle of the sea after them, all Pharaoh's horses, his chariots, and his horsemen.

When morning came, the Lord looked down on the host of the Egyptians through the pillar of fire and the cloud, and troubled the forces of the Egyptians. He made wheels fall off their chariots and made them drive heavily, so that the Egyptians said, "Let us flee from the children of Israel, for the Lord fights for them against the Egyptians."

Then the Lord said to Moses, "Stretch out your hand over the sea, so that the waters may come together again and cover the Egyptians, their chariots, and their horsemen."

Moses stretched out his hand over the sea, and the sea returned to its bed when morning appeared. The Egyptians fled before it, but the

Lord overthrew the Egyptians in the middle of the sea. The waters returned and covered the chariots and the horsemen and all the forces of Pharaoh that had followed him into the sea. Not one of them survived.

But the children of Israel had walked on dry ground in the middle of the sea, and the waters were a wall on their right hand and on their left. Thus the Lord saved Israel that day from the clutch of the Egyptians, and the Israelites saw the Egyptians dead upon the seashore.

When Israel saw the great work the Lord did against the Egyptians, the people stood in awe of the Lord, and believed in him and in his servant Moses.

Then Moses and the children of Israel sang this song to the Lord:

"I will sing to the Lord, for he has triumphed gloriously;
The horse and the rider he has thrown into the sea.
The Lord is my strength and song, and he has become my saviour;
He is my God, and I will prepare him a house;
He is my father's God, and I will exalt him."

And Miriam the prophetess, the sister of Aaron, took a timbrel in her hand, and all the women went out after her with timbrels and danced. And Miriam replied to them in song:

"Sing everyone to the Lord, for he has triumphed gloriously;
The horse and his rider he has thrown into the sea."

THE BITTER WELL OF MARAH

O MOSES led the Israelites from the Red Sea into the wilderness of Shur; and they went three days in the wilderness and found no water.

When at last they came unto Marah, they could not drink the water there, for it was bitter; that was why the name of the place was Marah. The people murmured against Moses, saying, "What shall we drink?"

He cried to the Lord, and the Lord showed him a tree which, when he cast it into the waters, made the waters sweet. And there the Lord also laid down a law for them. He said, "If you will listen carefully to the voice of the Lord your God, and will do what is right in his sight, and will give an ear to his commandments, and keep all his laws, I will not bring upon you any of those diseases which I brought upon the Egyptians, for I am the Lord who heals and protects you."

Then they came to Elim, where there were twelve wells of water and a grove of seventy palm trees, and they camped beside the waters.

MANNA FROM HEAVEN

ONWARD from Elim they journeyed, and all the congregation of the children of Israel came to the wilderness of Sin, which is between Elim and Sinai, on the fifteenth day of the second month after their departure from Egypt. And the children of Israel were murmuring against Moses and Aaron in the wilderness.

"It would have been better for us to perish by the hand of the Lord in the land of Egypt, when we sat down to bowls of meat and ate our fill of bread. For you have brought us out into this wilderness to kill the whole band of us with hunger."

Then the Lord said to Moses, "You will see, I will rain bread down from heaven for you. The people shall go out and gather a certain amount every day, so that I may test them, to see whether they will obey my laws or not. And it will be arranged so that on the sixth day they shall prepare what they bring in, which will be twice as much as they gather on other days."

Moses and Aaron said to all the children of Israel, "When evening comes, you will know that it is the Lord who has brought you out of the land of Egypt. And when morning comes, you will see the glory of the Lord. For he has heard your murmurings against him; your murmurings are not against us—for what are we?—but against the Lord."

And while Aaron was speaking to the congregation of the children of Israel, they looked out over the wilderness, and there they saw the glory of the Lord appear in the clouds.

Then the Lord spoke to Moses, saying, "I have heard the murmuring of the children of Israel. Speak to them and say: 'At evening you will eat meat, and in the morning you will have your fill of bread, and so you will know that I am the Lord your God.'"

And it came to pass that in the evening quails flew up all over the camp; and in the morning dew lay all around the people. And when the dew had disappeared, they saw lying on the face of the wilderness small round things, as small as hoarfrost, on the ground.

Moses said to them, "That is the bread which the Lord has sent for you to eat. And this is the commandment of the Lord: You are to gather an omer [about a tenth of a bushel] for each man, depending on how many you have to feed; each man is to gather for those in his tents."

So the children of Israel went out and gathered it. Some took more and some took less, but when they measured it with an omer, those who had gathered a great deal had nothing over, and those who had gathered little had no less; each man had enough to feed his people.

Moses said, "Do not leave any until morning."

Nevertheless they did not listen to Moses, and some of them left it until the next morning; and it bred worms and smelled foul. Then Moses was angry with them.

So they gathered it every morning, each man according to those he had to feed; and when the sun grew hot, it melted.

When the sixth day came, they gathered twice as much food, two omers for each man; and all the rulers of the congregation came to Moses for directions.

He said to them, "This is what the Lord has said: 'Tomorrow is the day of rest, the Lord's sabbath; bake what you want to bake today, and boil what you want to boil, and what is left you may save, to keep for tomorrow.'"

So they laid it away until morning as Moses told them to, and it did not smell bad, nor was there a single worm in it.

Moses said, "Eat that today, for today is the Lord's sabbath; today you will not find manna in the field. Six days you are to gather it, but on the seventh day, which is the sabbath, there will not be any."

And so it was: for some of the people went out on the seventh day to gather, and they found none.

Now the house of Israel called the name of the food *Manna;* and it was white like coriander seeds, and the taste of it was like wafers made with honey.

And the children of Israel ate manna forty years, until they came to the borders of the land of Canaan.

THE TEN COMMANDMENTS

T WAS in the third month after the children of Israel left Egypt that they came into the wilderness of Sinai. They pitched their tents in the wilderness and camped there before the mountain.

Moses went up to talk to God, and the Lord called to him from the mountain, saying: "Tell this to the children of Israel: 'You have seen what I did to the Egyptians, and how I lifted you up on eagles' wings and brought you to myself. Now, if you will really obey my voice and keep your agreement with me, then you will be a special treasure to me, more than any other people. You will be a kingdom of priests to me, and a holy nation.' This is what you are to tell the children of Israel."

Moses came down and called the elders of the people together, and laid before them all the words of the Lord. And the people answered together and said, "All that the Lord has said, we will do."

Then Moses told the Lord what the people had said.

Then the Lord said to Moses, "Lo, I will come to you in a thick cloud, so that the people may hear when I speak to you and believe forever.

"Now go to the people, and purify them today and tomorrow, and have them wash their clothes and be ready for the third day. For the third day the Lord will come down in the sight of all the people upon Mount Sinai. Set bounds for the people, and warn them to take care not to go up on the mountain or touch the edge of it, for whoever touches the mountain shall surely be put to death. Anyone who does touch it shall be stoned or shot; whether it be man or beast. But when the trumpet sounds a long blast, they shall come up to the mountain."

Then Moses went down from the mountain to the people, and he purified them, and they washed their clothes. And he said to the people, "Be ready for the third day."

The third day came at last, and in the morning there was thunder and lightning, and a thick cloud lay upon the mountain. Then the voice of the trumpet sounded so loud that all the people in the camp trembled.

Then Moses led the people out of the camp to meet with God, and they stood at the back of the mountain.

Mount Sinai was covered with smoke, because the Lord descended on it in fire; the smoke rose up like the smoke of a furnace, and the whole mountain trembled and shook.

When the voice of the trumpet sounded long blasts, and grew louder and louder, Moses spoke and God answered him in a voice. Then the Lord came down upon the top of Mount Sinai, and he called Moses up to the top of the mount, and Moses went up.

And God spoke all these words:

"I am the Lord your God, who has brought you out of the land of Egypt, out of the house of slavery. You shall have no other gods before me.

"You shall not make for yourselves any images carved to look like anything that is in heaven above, or on the earth beneath, or in the water under the earth.

"You shall not use the name of the Lord your God in any careless way.

"Remember the sabbath day, and keep it holy. Six days you shall work and accomplish all you must do, but the seventh day is the sabbath of the Lord your God; in it you must not do any work.

"Honor your father and your mother.

"You shall not kill.

"You shall not commit adultery.

"You shall not steal.

"You shall not bring false charges against anyone.

"You must not be greedy for what belongs to others."

All the people saw the thunder and lightning and heard the noise of the trumpet and saw the mountain smoke; and they were frightened and moved away, and waited at a distance.

They said to Moses, "You speak to us and we will listen; but do not let God speak to us, lest we die."

And Moses said to the people, "Do not fear, for God has come to test you, so that you may learn to have respect for him, so that you will not do wrong."

Then the people stood far off, while Moses drew near to the thick darkness where God was. And the Lord spoke to Moses and gave him laws to govern the tribes of Israel in all their acts.

MOSES *came down and told the people all the words of the Lord and all his laws, and the people answered and said, "Everything the Lord has said, we will do."*

Moses wrote down all the words of the Lord, and he arose early in the morning and built an altar to the Lord, with twelve pillars for the twelve tribes of Israel, and he sacrificed to the Lord.

Then, as the Lord had commanded, Moses took Aaron and seventy of the elders up on to the mountain.

But only Moses went up into the cloud which covered the top of the mountain, and he stayed forty days and forty nights, while the Lord gave him all the rules for the temple and the priests. And when the Lord had finished talking with him upon Mount Sinai, the Lord gave Moses two tablets of stone, bearing the laws written with the finger of God. These tablets were to be kept in a special box (known later as the Ark of the Covenant).

AARON MAKES THE GOLDEN CALF

 HEN the people saw that Moses was not coming down from the mountain at once, they gathered around Aaron and said to him, "Make us gods to lead us, for as for this Moses, the man who brought us up out of the land of Egypt, we do not know what has become of him."

Aaron said to them, "Break off the golden earrings which your wives and sons and daughters wear in their ears, and bring them to me."

So all the people broke off the golden earrings in their ears and brought them to Aaron. He took them from their hands and melted the gold and fashioned it with a tool into a golden calf.

"Let this be your god, O Israel, which brought you up out of the land of Egypt," they said.

When Aaron saw it, he built an altar before it; then he made a proclamation and said, "Tomorrow is a feast to the Lord."

They rose up early the next morning and offered burnt offerings and brought peace offerings, and the people sat down to eat and to drink and rose up to play.

Then the Lord said to Moses, "Go down there, for your people, whom you have brought out of the land of Egypt, have wandered from the right path; they have turned aside from the way I commanded them to go, and they have made themselves a golden calf and worshiped it. They have made sacrifices to it and said, 'These are your gods, O Israel, which brought you out of the land of Egypt.'" And the Lord said, "I have watched this people, and they are a stubborn people. Now leave me alone, for my anger has grown hot against them and I will destroy them and make a great nation of you alone."

Then Moses pleaded with the Lord his God, saying, "Lord, why are you angry against this people you have brought out of the land of Egypt by your great power and with your mighty hand? Do you want the Egyptians to be able to say, 'He led them out as a trick to slay them in the mountains and destroy them from the face of the earth'? Remember Abraham, Isaac, and Israel, your servants, to whom you swore by your own name that you would multiply their race as the stars of the heaven and give all this land you have spoken of to their children, so that they would inherit it forever."

So the Lord repented of the evil which he planned to do to his people.

Then Moses turned and went down from the mountain, with the two tablets of laws in his hand; the tablets were filled with writing on both sides and were the work of God, and the writing was the writing of God engraved upon the tablets.

There was a man with Moses named Joshua. When he heard the noise of the people as they shouted, he said to Moses, "There is noise of war in the camp."

But Moses said, "It is not the voice of those who shout for victory, nor those who cry out in defeat, but the noise of those who sing that I hear."

As soon as he came close to the camp, he saw the calf and the dancing, and Moses' anger grew hot, and he hurled down the tablets from his hands, and they broke at the foot of the mountain.

He took the calf which they had made and burned it in the fire and ground it to powder and strewed it upon the water and made the children of Israel drink of it.

And Moses said to Aaron, "What did the people do to you that made you lead them into such great wrongdoing?"

Aaron said, "Do not be so angry, my lord; you know the people, and how they turn to mischief. They said to me, 'Make us gods to lead us, for we do not know what has become of Moses who led us out of the land of Egypt.'"

Moses returned again to the Lord and said, "Oh, this people have done a great wrong, and have made idols of gold; yet, if you can, I ask you to forgive them; if not, I beg you to blot me entirely out of your book."

The Lord said to Moses, "Go down and get on your way again, you and the people you have led up out of the land of Egypt, to the land which I promised to Abraham, to Isaac, and to Jacob for their children. I will send an angel before you to the land flowing with milk and honey, for I will not go with you myself, because you are a stubborn people."

When the people heard these words they mourned, and not a man of them wore his ornaments.

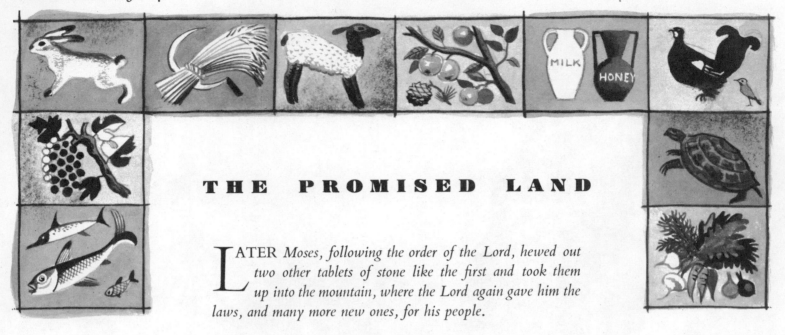

THE PROMISED LAND

LATER *Moses, following the order of the Lord, hewed out two other tablets of stone like the first and took them up into the mountain, where the Lord again gave him the laws, and many more new ones, for his people.*

SEND out men to look over the land of Canaan, which I am giving to the children of Israel," said the Lord, speaking to Moses. "Send a man from every tribe, and let each one be a ruler among his people."

Moses chose the men and sent them to spy out the land of Canaan, and said to them, "Start off to the south, and go up into the mountains, and see the land. See what it is like, and whether the people who dwell there are strong or weak, few or many. See what the land itself is like that they dwell in, whether it is good or bad, and what their cities are like, whether they live in tents or in strongholds. See whether the country is rich or poor, whether or not it has wood, and bring back some of the fruit of the land."

Now it was time for the first ripe grapes. When the men went up and searched the land, they came to the brook of Eshcol, and there they cut down a branch with one cluster of grapes and carried it between two of them upon a long staff; and they brought some pomegranates and some figs.

After forty days they returned from searching through the land; they came back to Moses and Aaron and all the congregation of the children of Israel at Kadesh in the wilderness of Paran, and brought word to them and showed them the fruit of the land.

"We came to the land you sent us to," they told Moses, "and it is indeed flowing with milk and honey, and this is the fruit of it. Nevertheless, the people are strong who dwell in the land, and the cities are walled and very large."

Caleb, one of the searchers, silenced the people and said, "Let us go up at once and take possession, for we are strong enough to overcome it."

But the other men who had gone up with him said, "We are not able to fight those people, for they are stronger than we." And they gave an evil report to the children of Israel on the land they had searched out, saying ,"The land which we went up to look over is a land that eats up its inhabitants. And all the people we saw in it are men of great height. And we saw there giants, the sons of Anak who was descended from giants; and we looked to ourselves like grasshoppers and were like grasshoppers in their sight."

Then all the congregation lifted up their voice and cried, and all the people wept that night.

The children of Israel murmured against Moses and Aaron, and the whole congregation said to them, "Would to God that we had died in the land of Egypt, or that we had died in the wilderness! Why has the Lord brought us to this land to fall by the sword, so that our wives and children will be captured? Would it not be better for us to return to Egypt?"

They said to one another, "Let us choose a captain and return to Egypt."

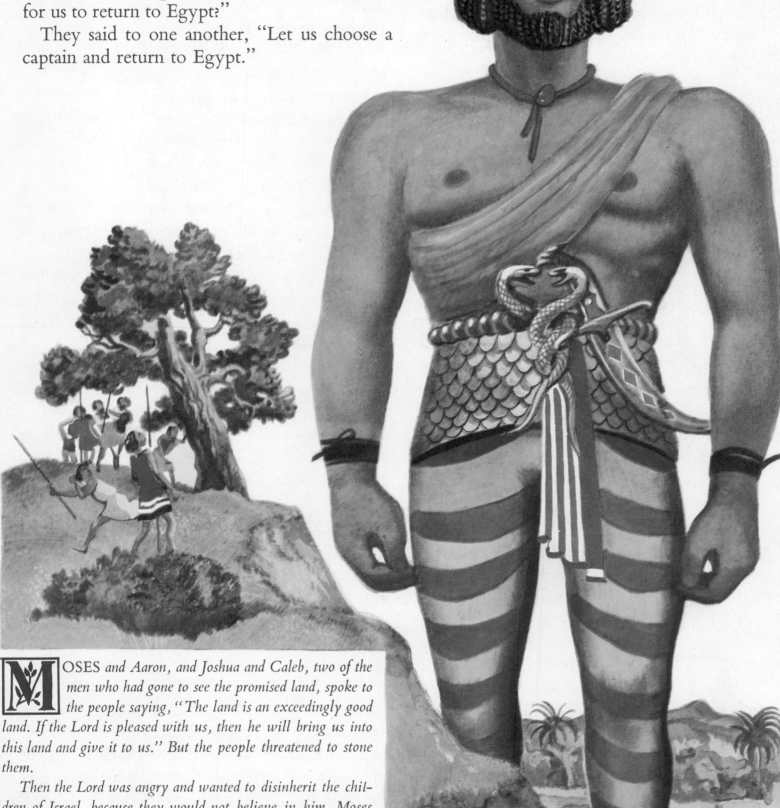

MOSES *and Aaron, and Joshua and Caleb, two of the men who had gone to see the promised land, spoke to the people saying, "The land is an exceedingly good land. If the Lord is pleased with us, then he will bring us into this land and give it to us." But the people threatened to stone them.*

Then the Lord was angry and wanted to disinherit the children of Israel, because they would not believe in him. Moses begged the Lord to forgive his people, and at last he did; but the Lord decreed that the children of Israel should wander in the desert for forty years before they could enter the promised land.

MOSES COMPLETES HIS WORK

WHEN *the forty years of wandering, with hardships and fighting, were over, Moses gathered the children of Israel together and reminded them of all the laws God had laid down for them and of their covenant with the Lord.*

Moses knew that when he was no longer there to lead them, the people would forget their duty to God and disobey his laws, so he wrote them a song, and taught it to them, to remind them of the Lord's love for them.

He gave a special blessing to each of the tribes of Israel, and he finished with these words:

HERE is none like the God of Israel, who rides upon the highest heavens in your behalf, and in his majesty rides upon the sky. The eternal God is your refuge, and beneath you are his everlasting arms. He shall push away the enemy from before you and shall say, 'Destroy them.' Then Israel shall dwell alone in safety; the fountain of Jacob shall be upon a land of corn and wine, and his heaven shall drop down dew.

"How happy you are, O Israel! Who is like you, O people saved by the Lord, the shield of your weakness and the sword of your power! You will find out the faults of your enemies and walk in the courts of their power."

Then Moses went up from the plain of Moab to the mountain of Nebo, to the peak of Pisgah over toward Jericho. The Lord showed him all the land he was giving to each of the tribes of Israel. He looked off to the farthest sea, and southward over the plain of the valley of Jericho, the city of palm trees, to Zoar.

And the Lord said to him, "This is the land which I promised to Abraham, to Isaac, and to Jacob; I have let you see it with your own eyes, but you shall not go over there."

So Moses, the servant of the Lord, died there in the land of Moab. They buried him in a valley in the land of Moab, near Bethpeor, but no man knows to this day where his grave lies. And Moses was a hundred and twenty years old when he died; but his eye was not dimmed, and his strength had not failed him.

The children of Israel wept for Moses in the plains of Moab thirty days. Then the days of weeping and mourning for Moses were over.

Now Joshua, the son of Nun, was full of the spirit of wisdom, for Moses had blessed him, and the children of Israel listened to his words and did as the Lord commanded. But never again in all Israel was there a prophet like Moses, whom the Lord knew face to face.

JOSHUA SENDS SPIES INTO CANAAN

AFTER the death of Moses, the Lord put Joshua in command of the children of Israel. "Be strong and of good courage," said the Lord. "Do not be afraid, and do not be dismayed; for the Lord your God is with you wherever you go."

Joshua commanded the officers of the people: "Go among the people and tell them to prepare food, for within three days we shall pass over the Jordan river to enter the land which the Lord our God has given us."

Then Joshua sent out two men to spy secretly, saying, "Go look over the land and Jericho." They went, and came to the house of a woman named Rahab and took a room there.

Then the king of Jericho was told, "Men came here in the night from the children of Israel, to look over our country."

The king of Jericho sent word to Rahab: "Bring out the men who came to you and are now in your house, for they have come to spy in our country."

The woman took the two men and hid them and said, "There were two men who came here, but I did not know where they had come from. And about the time of the shutting of the gate, when it was getting dark, the men went out. Where they were going I do not know, but if you pursue them quickly you will overtake them."

But really she had brought them up to the roof of the house and hidden them under stalks of flax which she had laid out on the roof.

Meanwhile the King's men searched for them all the way to the fords of the Jordan.

Before the men on the roof had settled themselves, Rahab came up and said, "I know that the Lord has given you the land, and that your terror hangs over us, and all the inhabitants of the land faint because of you. For we have heard how the Lord dried up the water of the Red Sea for you when you came out of Egypt, and as soon as we heard that, our hearts melted, and not a man had any courage left, all because of you. For the Lord your God is God in heaven above and in the earth beneath."

W HEN *she asked them to spare her family's lives in return for her helping them escape, the men agreed. They said to her:*

"When the children of Israel come into the land, you tie a bit of scarlet cloth in the window, and bring your father and mother and your brothers and all your father's household into your house. Then if anyone goes out from your house into the street, whatever happens to him will be his own fault, and we shall not be guilty; but we will be responsible for whoever stays with you in the house, to see that no one touches him. But if you say a word about our business here, then we will no longer keep our promise."

"It shall be just as you say," she said. Then she sent them away, and after they had left she tied the bit of scarlet in the window.

The two men went back down the mountain and crossed the river and came back to Joshua, the son of Nun, and told him all the things that had happened. And they said to Joshua, "Truly the Lord has delivered all the country into our hands, for all the people of the land faint with fear of us."

THE FALL OF JERICHO

JERICHO, that great city, was tightly shut up, because of the children of Israel; no one went out of the city, and no one came in. Then the Lord told Joshua how he and his people could capture the city, and Joshua called the priests and the people and gave them their orders.

It came to pass, when Joshua had spoken to the people, that seven priests bearing seven trumpets made of rams' horns went forward before the ark of the Lord and blew on the trumpets, and the ark followed them. The armed men went before the priests blowing on trumpets, and the rear guard came after the ark.

Now Joshua had commanded the people, "You shall not shout nor make any noise with your voices, nor shall any word come out of your mouths until the day when I bid you to shout. Then you shall shout."

So the ark of the Lord circled the city, going about it once. Then they came back to the camp and stayed there.

Next day Joshua rose up early in the morning, and the priests took up the ark of the Lord. Again seven priests, bearing seven trumpets of rams' horns before the ark of the Lord, went steadily ahead, blowing on the trumpets; and the armed guard went before them; but the rear guard came after the ark of the Lord.

The second day they circled the city once and returned to the camp; this they did for six days.

It came to pass on the seventh day that they rose early, about the dawning of the day, and circled the city in the same way seven times. On that one day they circled the city seven times.

At the seventh time, while the priests blew on their trumpets, Joshua said to the people, "Shout, for the Lord has given you the city."

So the people shouted while the priests blew on their trumpets; and when the people heard the sound of the trumpet and shouted with a great shout, the wall fell down flat, so that the people went into the city, each man walking straight ahead, and they took the city.

AFTERWARD *Joshua took the whole land, according to all that the Lord had said to Moses, and Joshua gave it for an inheritance to Israel, according to their division by tribes. Then the land rested from war.*

GIDEON AND THE MIDIANITES

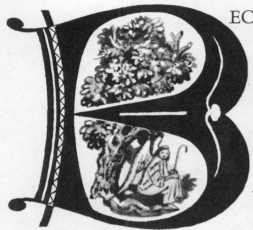

BECAUSE the children of Israel did evil in the sight of the Lord, the Lord gave the Midianites power over them for seven years.

When the seven years were up, there came an angel of the Lord and sat under a certain oak in Ophrah, which belonged to Joash the Abiezrite. His son Gideon was threshing wheat by the winepress, to hide it from the Midianites.

The angel of the Lord appeared to him and said to him, "The Lord is with you, you mighty man of valor."

Gideon said to him, "Oh, my Lord, if the Lord is with us, why has all this happened to us? Where are all his miracles, of which our fathers told us? The Lord has forsaken us now and has given us up to the Midianites."

Then the angel looked at him and said, "Go out in your strength, and you shall save Israel from the Midianites. Have I not sent you?"

"If I have found favor in your sight," Gideon said to him, "show me a sign that it is you who are talking with me. Stay here until I come back and bring a present and set it before you."

"I will wait here until you come again," the angel said.

So Gideon went in and prepared a kid and unleavened cakes of a measure of flour. The meat he put in a basket, and he put the broth in a pot and brought it out to the angel under the oak, and presented it.

The angel of God said to him, "Take the meat and the unleavened cakes and lay them upon this rock and pour out the broth."

Gideon did so.

Then the angel of the Lord stretched out the end of the staff that was in his hand and touched the meat and the unleavened cakes, and fire rose up out of the rock and consumed the meat and the unleavened cakes. And the angel of the Lord disappeared from sight.

When Gideon saw that this was indeed an angel of the Lord, he said, "Alas, O Lord God! I am frightened because I have seen an angel of the Lord face to face."

The Lord said to him, "Be at peace, and do not be afraid; you shall not die."

Then Gideon built an altar there to the Lord, and called it Jehovahshalom. To this day it stands in Ophrah of the Abiezrites.

THE TRUMPETS AND THE LAMPS

GIDEON gathered an army of the people of Israel behind him. They pitched their tents beside the well of Harod, so that the ranks of the Midianites were off to the north of them, by the hill of Moreh, in the valley.

The Lord said to Gideon, "The people with you are too many for me to give them a victory over the Midianites, for then Israel might boast of its own power, saying, 'Our own hands have saved us.' Go to the people, therefore, and tell everyone who is fearful and afraid to go back, and leave Mount Gilead."

Twenty-two thousand of the people returned, and ten thousand stayed.

Then the Lord said to Gideon, "There are still too many people. Bring them down to the water, and I will test them for you. If I say, 'This one shall go with you,' he shall go with you, and if I say, 'This one shall not go with you,' he shall not go."

So Gideon brought the people down to the water, and the Lord said to Gideon, "Set apart those who lap the water with their tongues, as a dog laps, and those who kneel down to drink."

The number of those who lapped, putting their hands to their mouths, was three hundred men; but all the rest of the people bowed down upon their knees to drink water.

Then the Lord said to Gideon, "By the three hundred men who lapped I will save you and will deliver the Midianites into your hands; let all the other people go to their homes."

So the chosen people took food in their hands, and their trumpets, and Gideon sent all the rest of the Israelites to their tents and kept only those three hundred men. And the army of Midian was beneath, in the valley.

That same night the Lord said to Gideon, "Arise, go down to the camp, for I have given it into your hands. But if you are afraid to go down, take your servant Phurah down with you; you will hear what they are saying, and afterwards your hands will be strengthened for the battle."

Then Gideon went down with Phurah his servant to the outermost of the armed men that were in the camp. There the Midianites and the Amalekites, and all the children of the east, lay along the valley like grasshoppers in their numbers, and their camels were countless, as many as the sand by the seaside.

When Gideon came near, a man was telling a dream to his companion; and he said, "I just dreamed a dream, and in it a cake of barley bread tumbled into the camp of Midian. It came to a tent and struck it so that it fell and over-turned, so that the tent lay flat on the ground."

His companion answered and said, "This is nothing else than the sword of Gideon, the son of Joash, a man of Israel. For God is giving him a victory over Midian and all the army."

When Gideon heard the telling of the dream and the interpretation of it, he worshiped God; then he returned to the army of Israel and said, "Arise, for the Lord has given into your hands the army of Midian."

He divided the three hundred men into three companies, and he put a trumpet into every man's hand, and gave them empty pitchers with lights inside them.

"Watch me and do likewise," he said to them; "and see that when I come to the outskirts of the camp, you do just what I do. When I blow on a trumpet, I and those who are with me, then you blow on the trumpet too, on every side of the whole camp, and shout, 'The sword of the Lord and of Gideon!' "

So Gideon and the hundred men who were with him came to the outskirts of the camp in the beginning of the middle watch, when a new watch had just been posted. Then they blew on their trumpets and broke the pitchers that were in their hands. And the three companies all blew on their trumpets and broke the pitchers and held the lights in their left hands and the trumpets in their right hands. And they cried, "The sword of the Lord and of Gideon!"

They stood, every man in his place, round about the camp, and all the army of Midian cried out and fled.

The three hundred blew on their trumpets, and through the whole army of the Midianites the Lord made men turn their swords one against another, and the army fled to Beth-shittah in Zererath, and to Tabbath on the border of Abelmeholah.

THE PARABLE OF THE TREES

IDEON *died, leaving seventy sons. One son, Abimelech, killed all his brothers but the youngest, Jotham, who hid himself. Then Abimelech made himself king.*

OTHAM heard of this and he went and stood on the top of Mount Gerizim, and lifted up his voice, and cried, "Listen to me, you men of Shechem, that God may listen to you.

"The trees went forth once upon a time to choose a king, and they said to the olive tree, 'Rule over us.'

"But the olive tree said to them, 'Should I leave my richness, which is such that they honor God and man with my branches, and go to rule over the trees?'

"Then the trees said to the fig tree, 'You come and rule over us.'

"But the fig tree said to them, 'Should I forsake my sweetness, and my good fruit, and go to be king over the trees?'

"Then the trees said to the vine, 'You come and rule over us.'

"And the vine said to them, 'Should I leave my wine, which cheers God and man, and go to be king over the trees?'

"Then all the trees said to the worthless bramble, 'You come and rule over us.'

"And the bramble said to the trees, 'If you really appoint me king over you, then come and put your trust in me, and if not, let fire come out of the bramble and devour the cedars of Lebanon.'"

(Things happened just as Jotham's story suggested. Abimelech did turn upon and destroy the men who had made him king.)

SAMSON AND HIS MIGHTY STRENGTH

NOW *Samson was the son of Manoah, of the family of the Danites. Before he was born, an angel of the Lord appeared to his parents to tell them that he was to be consecrated to God, and was never to drink wine or cut his hair. Samson grew up to be a powerful young man who killed a lion with his bare hands, and with the jawbone of an ox slew a thousand of the Philistines, who were enemies of the Israelites.*

SAMSON loved a woman in the valley of Sorek, whose name was Delilah. The leaders of the Philistines came to her and said to her, "Coax him and learn what gives him his great strength, and by what means we may triumph over him, so that we may bind him and humble him; for this we will give you, every one of us, eleven hundred pieces of silver."

So Delilah said to Samson, "Tell me, I beg you, what gives you your great strength, and how you could be bound to be made helpless."

"If anyone bound me with seven green willow stems that have never been dried, I should be as weak as any other man," Samson said to her.

Then the leaders of the Philistines brought to her seven green willow stems which had not been dried, and she bound him with them.

Now there were men lying in wait, waiting with her in the chamber. And she said to Samson, "The Philistines are upon you, Samson!"

Then he broke the stems as a strand of hemp is broken when it touches the fire; so the secret of his strength was not known.

Delilah said to Samson, "See, you have

mocked me and told me lies. Now tell me, I beg you, with what could you be securely bound?"

And he said to her, "If they bind me fast with new ropes that have never been used, then I shall be weak and just like any other man."

Delilah therefore took new ropes and bound him with them and said to him, "The Philistines are upon you, Samson!"

For again there were men lying in wait in

the chamber. But Samson broke the ropes from his arms like a thread.

Delilah said again to Samson, "Up to now you have mocked me and told me lies. Tell me now with what you could really be bound."

And he said to her, "Weave the seven locks of my hair with the web of cloth on your loom."

She did so while he slept, and fastened it with the pin of the loom. Then she said to him, "The Philistines are upon you, Samson!"

But he waked out of his sleep and carried away the pin of the loom and the web of cloth.

Then she said to him, "How can you say 'I love you,' when you do not trust me in your heart? Three times now you have mocked me and have not told me what the secret of your great strength is."

She kept on entreating him every day with her words, and when she had urged him, so that he was annoyed to desperation, he told her all that was in his heart.

"A razor has never touched my head," he said to her, "for I have been consecrated to God, a Nazarite, since before I was born. If I were shaved, my strength would go from me, and I would become weak and be like any other man."

When Delilah saw that he had told her the secret of his heart, she sent out a call for the lords of the Philistines, saying, "Come up once more, for he has told me the secret of his heart."

Then the lords of the Philistines came up to her, bringing the money in their hands.

Meanwhile she made Samson go to sleep on her knees; then she called for a man and had him shave off the seven locks of Samson's hair. By that she humbled him, for his strength went from him.

Then she said, "The Philistines are upon you, Samson!"

He awoke from his sleep, and said, "I will go out, as I did the other times, and shake myself." For he did not know that the power of the Lord was gone from him.

But quickly the Philistines took him, and put out his eyes, and took him down to Gaza. There they bound him with fetters of brass and made him grind in the prison house.

Gradually the hair of his head began to grow again. But the Philistines did not notice. They gathered together to offer a great sacrifice to Dagon, their god, and to rejoice; for they said, "Our God has delivered Samson our enemy into our hands."

When they saw Samson, they praised their god; for they said, "Our god has delivered into our hands our enemy and the destroyer of our country, who has slain many of us."

It happened that, while the hearts of the people were merry, they said, "Call Samson out, so that he can entertain us." So they brought Samson up out of the prison house and made fun of him.

When they stood him up between two pillars, Samson said to the boy who held him by the hand, "Let me feel the pillars which support the house, so that I may lean upon them."

Now the house was full of men and women, and all the leaders of the Philistines were there; and there were about three thousand men and women on the roof, watching while Samson was made fun of.

Then Samson called out to the Lord and said, "O Lord God, remember me, I pray you, and strengthen me, I pray you, only this once, O God, that I may take revenge on the Philistines for my two eyes."

Then Samson took hold of the two middle pillars upon which the house stood, and which held it up; he held one with his right hand, and the other with his left.

Samson said, "Let me die with the Philistines." And he bowed himself with all his might, and the house fell upon all the people who were inside; so the number he killed at his death was greater than he had killed in his life.

Then his brothers, and all the household of his father, came down and took his body. And they took him home, and buried him between Zorah and Eshtaol, in the burying place of Manoah his father.

RUTH, THE FAITHFUL DAUGHTER-IN-LAW

IT happened, in the old days when the judges ruled Israel, that there was a famine in the land. And a certain man of Bethlehemjudah went to stay in the country of Moab, he and his wife and his two sons. The name of the man was Elimelech, and the name of his wife was Naomi, and his two sons were Mahlon and Chilion. They came into the country of Moab and stayed there.

Elimelech, Naomi's husband, died, and she was left with her two sons. They took wives of the women of Moab; the name of the one was Orpah, and the name of the other Ruth. They lived there about ten years.

Then Mahlon and Chilion both died, and their mother was left without husband or sons. She arose, with her daughters-in-law, to return home from the country of Moab, for she had heard in the country of Moab how the Lord had visited his people and given them food again. Therefore she left the place where she was, with her two daughters-in-law, and they started to go back to the land of Judah.

But Naomi said to her two daughters-in-law, "Go, return each of you to her mother's house. May the Lord be as kind to you as you have been to the dead and to me."

They lifted up their voices and wept; and Orpah kissed her mother-in-law, but Ruth clung to her.

And Naomi said to Ruth, "See, your sister-in-law has gone back to her people and to her gods. You go after your sister-in-law."

But Ruth said, "Do not ask me to leave you or to go back instead of following after you; for where you go, I will go; and where you stop, I will stop; your people shall be my people, and your God my God. Where you die I will die, and there I will be buried. The Lord punish me and more, if anything but death part me from you!"

When Naomi saw that Ruth was determined to go with her, she agreed. So the two traveled on until they came to Bethlehem. They reached Bethlehem at the beginning of the barley harvest.

Now Naomi had a kinsman of her husband's, a mighty man of great wealth, of the family of Elimelech; and his name was Boaz.

Ruth the Moabitess said to Naomi, "Let me go now to the fields and glean ears of grain after whoever gives me his approval to do so."

And Naomi said to her, "Go, my daughter."

So Ruth came to the field and gleaned after the reapers; and it was her luck to light on a part of the field belonging to Boaz, who was the kin of Elimelech.

It happened that Boaz came from Bethlehem and said to the reapers, "The Lord be with you."

And they answered him, "The Lord bless you."

Then Boaz said to the servant who was in charge of the reapers, "Whose girl is that?"

The servant in charge of the reapers answered and said, "It is the Moabitish girl who came back with Naomi from the country of Moab. She asked permission to glean and gather after the reapers among the sheaves, so she came and has worked since morning, until just now when she rested a little in the shelter."

Then Boaz said to Ruth, "Do you hear me, my daughter? Do not go to glean in another field, nor go away from here, but stay close by my maidservants. Watch the field where they reap and follow them. I have ordered the servants not to touch you. And when you are thirsty, go to the water jars and drink from the water which the young men have drawn."

Then she fell on her face and bowed herself to the ground and said to him, "Why have I found favor in your eyes, that you should take notice of me, seeing that I am a stranger?"

Boaz answered and said to her, "I have heard all that you have done for your mother-in-law since the death of your husband, and how you have left your father and mother and the land of your birth, and have come to a people you had never known before. May the Lord repay your good deeds, and may a full reward be given you by the Lord God of Israel, under whose wings you have come to rest."

Then she said, "Let me find favor in your sight, my lord; for you have comforted me by speaking friendly words to your handmaid, though I am not really one of your handmaids."

And Boaz said to her, "At mealtime come here and eat of the bread, and dip your piece into the sauce."

So she sat beside the reapers, and he passed her parched grain, and she ate until she had had enough, and then left.

When she arose to glean again, Boaz gave orders to his young men, saying, "Let her glean even among the sheaves, and do not reproach her. And also let fall some handfuls on purpose for her, and leave them so that she may glean them, and do not stop her."

So she gleaned in the field until evening, and threshed out what she had gleaned, and it was about an ephah of barley.

She gathered it up and went into the city and showed her mother-in-law what she had gleaned.

Her mother-in-law said to her, "Where did

you glean today? Where did you work? Blessed be he that took notice of you."

She told her mother-in-law with whom she had worked, saying, "The man's name with whom I worked today is Boaz."

Then Naomi said to her daughter-in-law, "May the Lord bless him, for the Lord has not stopped showing kindness to the living and the dead." And she added, "The man is near of kin to us, one of our next kinsmen."

Ruth the Moabitess said, "He told me, too, to stay near his young men until they have finished his harvest."

And Naomi said to Ruth her daughter-in-law, "It is good that you go out with his maid-servants, so that you do not go into any other field."

So she stayed close by the maidens of Boaz to glean until the end of barley harvest and of wheat harvest; and she lived with her mother-in-law.

Ruth *the Moabitess pleased Boaz very much. When the harvest was over he went to the gate where the elders of the city sat, and, according to the custom of the Israelites, he announced that he wanted to marry Ruth. All the people who were at the gate wished them well, and gave them a blessing. So they were married, and Ruth bore a son. Then Naomi was happy again, and she became the child's nurse. They called the child Obed, and he became the father of Jesse, who was the father of David.*

SAMUEL, CHILD OF THE LORD

ONCE there was a woman named Hannah who was bitter in her soul because she had no sons or daughters. She prayed to the Lord and wept sadly. And she vowed a vow:

"O Lord of hosts, if you will look down upon the sadness of your handmaiden and remember me, and will give to your handmaiden a man-child, then I will give him to the Lord all the days of his life, and no razor shall touch his head."

It came to pass in due time that Hannah bore a son, and she called him Samuel, "because," she said, "I asked him of the Lord."

Her husband Elkanah, and all his household, went up to offer to the Lord the yearly sacrifice. But Hannah did not go, for she said to her husband, "I will not go up until the child is weaned, and then I will take him so that he may appear before the Lord and stay there forever."

Elkanah her husband said to her, "Do what seems best to you; wait until you have weaned him; only keep your word to the Lord." So the woman stayed home and nursed her son until he was old enough to wean.

When she had weaned him, she took him up with her, with three bullocks and one measure of flour and a bottle of wine, and brought him to the house of the Lord in Shiloh, when the child was still very young.

They slew a bullock and brought the child to Eli the priest. And Hannah said, "O my Lord, I am the woman who stood in the temple here, praying to the Lord. I prayed for this child, and the Lord has given me what I asked of him. Therefore I have lent him to the Lord. As long as he lives, he shall be lent to the Lord."

Then they worshiped the Lord there. And when Elkanah and his household went home, Samuel stayed, and was taught by Eli the priest.

Each year Samuel's mother made him a little coat and brought it to him when she came up with her husband to offer the yearly sacrifice.

And the child Samuel grew, and was in favor both with the Lord and with men. And he ministered to the Lord before Eli.

Eli's eyes began to grow dim, so that he could not see. Once when Eli was lying down in his place, before the lamp of God was put out in the temple where the ark of the Lord was kept, and before Samuel had lain down to sleep, the Lord called Samuel.

Samuel answered, "Here I am." He ran to Eli and said, "Here I am; you called me."

Eli said, "I did not call. Lie down and sleep."

He went and lay down, and again the Lord called, "Samuel."

Samuel arose and went to Eli and said, "Here I am, for you called me."

And Eli answered, "I did not call, my son; lie down again."

Now Samuel did not yet recognize the Lord, nor had the voice of the Lord been made known to him.

The Lord called Samuel again the third time, and he arose and went to Eli and said, "Here I am, for you called me."

Then Eli understood that the Lord had called the child. So Eli said to Samuel, "Go and lie down, and if he calls you, you are to say, 'Speak, Lord, for your servant is listening.'"

So Samuel went and lay down in his place.

The Lord came, and stood there, and called as at the other times, "Samuel, Samuel."

Then Samuel answered, "Speak, for your servant is listening."

And the Lord said to Samuel, "Behold, I am going to do something in Israel at which the ears of every one who hears it shall tingle. On an appointed day I will perform against Eli all the things I have spoken of concerning his household" (for Eli's sons were very wicked); "and when I begin I shall finish it. For I have told him that I will judge his house for ever for the wickedness of which he knows, because his sons made themselves evil, and he did not stop them. Therefore I have sworn to the house of Eli that their wickedness shall not be cleansed with sacrifices nor offerings for ever."

Samuel lay until morning; then he opened the doors of the house of the Lord, but he feared to tell Eli of the vision. Then Eli called Samuel and said, "Samuel, my son."

And he answered, "Here I am."

And he said, "What was it that the Lord said to you? I beg you not to hide it from me. May God punish you, and more, if you hide anything from me of the things that he said to you."

So Samuel told him everything, and hid nothing from him.

Eli said, "It is the Lord; let him do whatever seems good to him."

Samuel grew, and the Lord was with him. And all Israel, from Dan to Beersheba, knew that Samuel was established to be a prophet of the Lord.

DAVID, THE LORD'S CHOSEN ONE

FOR many years the tribes of Israel had been ruled by judges, but now the elders of the children of Israel gathered themselves together and asked Samuel to choose a king to rule over them. The Lord did not approve, for he felt the people would be poorer under a king and would come to regret it.

Nevertheless the people refused to obey the advice of Samuel, and they said, "Still we want a king over us."

So Samuel went out among the people of Israel and chose young Saul, a Benjamite, who was out with his servant hunting for his father's asses which were lost. Samuel took a vial of oil and poured it upon Saul's head and kissed him, and said, "The Lord has chosen you to be the captain of his people."

Saul was a handsome young man, head and shoulders taller than any of his fellows, and he became the first king over the children of Israel, and led them into many battles against their enemies, the Philistines.

But after a while, Saul disobeyed the laws of the Lord, so that the Lord was sorry he had made Saul king over Israel.

THE Lord said to Samuel, "How long will you mourn for Saul, seeing I have rejected him from reigning over Israel? Fill your horn with oil and go; I will send you to Jesse of Bethlehem, for I have chosen a king from among his sons."

Samuel did as the Lord told him and came to Bethlehem; and the elders of the town trembled at his coming and said, "Do you come peaceably?"

"Peaceably," he said. "I have come to sacrifice to the Lord. Make yourselves ready and come with me to the sacrifice."

He blessed Jesse and his sons and called them to the sacrifice.

When they came, he looked at Eliab and said, "Surely the Lord's chosen one is before him now."

But the Lord said to Samuel, "Do not look at his face or the height of him, because I have refused him. For the Lord does not see as man sees; man looks on the outward appearance, but the Lord looks at the heart."

Then Jesse called Abinadab and made him pass before Samuel; but Samuel said, "The Lord has not chosen this one either."

Then Jesse made Shammah pass by, and Samuel said, "Neither has the Lord chosen this one."

One after the other, Jesse made seven of his sons pass before Samuel. And Samuel said to Jesse, "The Lord has not chosen these." Then he asked, "Are all your children here?"

And Jesse said, "There is still the youngest, David. He is keeping the sheep."

Samuel said to Jesse, "Send and fetch him here, for we will not sit down until he comes."

David was sent for, and soon appeared. He was a rosy, healthy boy, and handsome.

The Lord said to Samuel, "Arise, anoint him, for this is he."

Then Samuel took the horn of oil and anointed David in the midst of his brothers. And the spirit of the Lord was with David from that day on.

DAVID MEETS SAUL, THE KING

AND the Spirit of the Lord departed from Saul, and an evil spirit troubled him.

Then Saul's servants said to him, "You see, an evil spirit from God is sent to trouble you. Now if you will command your servants, who are here before you, to find a man who is a cunning player on a harp, then when the evil spirit comes from God, he will play upon the strings, and you will be well."

"Find me a man who can play well," said Saul to his servants, "and bring him to me."

Then one of the servants answered and said, "I have seen a son of Jesse the Bethlehemite, who is clever at playing and a mighty courageous man, a man of war, sensible about business, a handsome person, and the Lord is with him."

Therefore Saul sent messengers to Jesse, and said, "Send me your son David, who is out with the sheep."

Jesse took an ass loaded with food, and a bottle of wine, and a kid, and sent them by David his son to Saul. And David came to Saul and stood before him, and served him.

David became very fond of Saul and was made the king's armorbearer. Then Saul sent word to Jesse, saying, "Let David stay with me, for he pleases me very much."

And it was true that when the evil spirit from God came upon Saul, David took a harp and played upon the strings, and Saul was refreshed and felt well again, and the evil spirit departed from him.

DAVID AND GOLIATH

OW the Philistines gathered their forces for battle. They gathered at Shochoh, and they camped in Ephesdammin.

Saul and the men of Israel were gathered together and camped in the valley of Elah, lined up in battle array against the Philistines.

The Philistines stood on a mountain on one side, and Israel stood on a mountain on the other side, and there was a valley between them.

Out from the camp of the Philistines came a champion named Goliath of Gath, whose height was nine feet and nine inches. He had a helmet of brass upon his head, and he was armed with a coat of mail, and the weight of the coat was five thousand shekels of brass. He had plates of brass upon his legs, and a shield of brass between his shoulders. The staff of his spear was like a weaver's beam, and his spear's head weighed six hundred shekels of iron. A shield bearer walked before him.

Goliath stood and cried out to the armies of Israel, "Why have you come out to set up your armies in battle array? Am I not a Philistine, and you servants of Saul? Choose a man to represent you, and let him come down to me. If he can fight me and kill me, then we will be your servants, but if I win over him and kill him, then you shall be our servants and serve us." And the Philistine said, "I defy the armies of Israel this day: send me a man, that we may fight together!"

When Saul and all the Israelites heard those words of the Philistine, they were dismayed and very much frightened. And every morning and evening for forty days, the Philistine drew near and challenged the Israelites.

David meanwhile had left the court of Saul to go home and feed his father's sheep at Bethlehem. His three eldest brothers were in the army of Saul.

Now Jesse said to David his son, "Take a measure of this parched grain and these ten loaves for your brothers and run to your brothers' camp. Carry these ten cheeses to the captain of their group, and see how your brothers are getting along."

David rose up early in the morning and left the sheep with a keeper, and started off as Jesse had commanded him. He came to the battle line just as the army was going out to the fight, shouting their battle cry. For Israel and the Philistines had put the army in battle array, army against army.

David left his baggage in the hands of the keeper of the baggage and ran among the army; he came up to his brothers and saluted them.

As he talked with them, up came the champion, Goliath of Gath, out of the armies of the Philistines, and he spoke his usual words, and David heard them.

All the men of Israel, when they saw the man, fled from him and were terribly afraid. "Have you seen this man who came up?" the men of Israel said. "He has come up to challenge Israel, and to the man who can kill him, the king will give great riches, and he will give him his daughter in marriage, and will make his father's house free in Israel."

And David spoke to the men standing near him, saying, "Who is this heathen Philistine, that he should challenge the armies of the living God?"

Eliab, his oldest brother, heard him speak to the men, and Eliab's anger was kindled against David, and he said, "Why did you come down here? With whom did you leave those few sheep in the wilderness? I know your pride, and the wickedness of your heart, for you have come down just so that you might see the battle."

David said, "What have I done now? Is there not a reason?" He turned from him toward another man and spoke to him in the same way, and the people answered him again just as before.

And when people heard the words which David spoke, they repeated them before Saul, and he sent for the boy.

But David said to Saul, "Let no man's heart be troubled because of Goliath. I, your servant, will go and fight with this Philistine."

Saul said, "You are not able to go out to fight with this Philistine, for you are but a boy, and he has been a man of war since his youth."

David said to Saul, "Your servant kept his father's sheep, and a lion came, and a bear, and took a lamb out of the flock. I went after him, and struck him down, and rescued it out of his mouth, and when he arose against me, I caught him by his beard and struck him and killed him. Your servant killed both the lion and the bear, and this heathen Philistine will be as one of them, seeing that he has challenged the armies of the living God."

Moreover, David said, "The Lord who saved me from the paw of the lion and from the paw of the bear, he will save me from the hand of this Philistine."

Then Saul said to David, "Go, and the Lord be with you."

Saul armed David with his armor, and he put a helmet of brass upon his head, and clothed him in a coat of mail. David fastened Saul's sword upon his armor and tried to walk, for he had not yet tried it. Then David said to Saul, "I cannot fight with these, for I am not used to them." And he took them off.

He took his staff in his hand, and chose five smooth stones out of the brook, and put them in a shepherd's bag which he had, and with his sling in his hand he drew near to the Philistine.

The Philistine came on and drew near to David, and the shield bearer went before him. But when the Philistine looked and saw David, he scorned him, for he was but a boy, rosy and fair of face.

The Philistine said to David, "Am I a dog, that you come to fight me with sticks?" And the Philistine cursed David by his gods.

Then David said to the Philistine, "You come to me with a sword and with a spear and with a shield, but I come to you in the name of the Lord of hosts, the God of the army of Israel, whom you have challenged. This day the Lord will put you into my hands, and I will strike you down and take your head from you, and I will give the bodies of the army of the Philistines to the birds of the air and to the wild beasts of the earth, so that all the earth may know that there is a God in Israel. And everyone gathered here will know that the Lord saves not with sword and spear, but the battle is the Lord's and he will give you into our hands."

Then, as the Philistine rose up and came nearer to meet David, David hurried and ran toward the army to meet the Philistine. And he put his hand in his bag and took out a stone, and slung it, and hit the Philistine in his forehead, so that the stone sank into his forehead and he fell upon his face on the earth.

So David triumphed over the Philistine with a sling and with a stone, and struck down the Philistine and killed him; but there was no sword in David's hand. Therefore David ran and stood upon the Philistine and took his sword and drew it out of its sheath, and killed him and cut off his head with it.

When the Philistines saw that their champion was dead, they fled. And the men of Israel arose, shouting, and pursued the Philistines all the way to the valley, to the gates of Ekron.

THE FRIENDSHIP OF DAVID AND JONATHAN

S AUL *took David home that day and would not let him go back to his father's house any more, and David and Jonathan, the son of Saul, became the best of friends.*

But it happened as they came along, when David was returning from the slaughter of the Philistine, that the women came out with joy from all the cities of Israel, singing and dancing, to meet King Saul, with tabrets and other musical instruments. And the women sang to one another as they played, and said, "Saul has killed his thousands and David his ten thousands." That displeased Saul, and he eyed David with suspicion from that day forward. Saul was afraid of David because the Lord was with him and had departed from Saul.

Twice, when the evil spirit was upon Saul, he tried to kill David, but still Jonathan loved David and protected him with his loyalty.

At last it was necessary for David to flee from the court, to be safe from Saul's anger, but still David and Jonathan swore to be friends forever.

O NE day Jonathan said to David, "Tomorrow is the feast of the new moon, and you will be missed, because your seat will be empty. When you have stayed away three days, come down quickly and wait by the stone Ezel.

"I will shoot three arrows beside the stone, as

if I shot at a target. And watch, I will send a boy, saying, 'Go, find the arrows.' If I expressly say to the boy, 'See, the arrows are on this side of you, pick them up,' then you come out, for there will be peace and no harm will be done to you, as the Lord lives.

"But if I say to the young man, 'See, the arrows are beyond you,' go your way, for the Lord will have sent you away.

"And about the matter of which we have spoken, may the Lord be between you and me for ever."

So David hid himself in the field.

When the moon had come, the king sat down to the feast. The king sat upon his seat, as always, a seat along the wall, and Jonathan arose, and Abner sat beside Saul, but David's place was empty.

Still Saul did not say anything that day

But it happened on the next day, which was the second day of the month, that David's place was empty again, and Saul said to Jonathan his son, "Why did the son of Jesse not come to dinner either yesterday or today?"

And Jonathan answered, "David earnestly asked permission of me to go to Bethlehem, for he said his family was to have a sacrifice there and his brother had bidden him to come, and he was eager to see all his brothers. That is why he did not come to the king's table."

Then Saul's anger was kindled against Jonathan, and he said to him, "You son of a perverse, rebellious woman, do I not know that you have chosen the son of Jesse to your own downfall? For as long as he lives, you shall not be established in the kingdom. Now send and fetch him to me, for he must die."

But Jonathan answered Saul his father, and said to him, "Why should he be slain? What has he done?"

Then Saul threw a javelin at him to strike him, and by that Jonathan knew that his father was determined to kill David. So Jonathan arose from the table in fierce anger and ate no dinner the second day of the month, for he was grieving for David.

In the morning Jonathan went out into the field at the time he had set with David, taking a little boy with him.

He said to the lad, "Run and hunt for the arrows which I am going to shoot." And, as the lad ran, he shot an arrow beyond him.

When the lad had come to the place where the arrow fell, Jonathan cried out to the lad and said, "Is the arrow not beyond you?" And again he cried, "Make speed, hasten, do not delay!"

Jonathan's lad took up the fallen arrow and came to his master, but the lad did not understand the thing: only Jonathan and David knew of the matter.

Then Jonathan gave his weapons to the lad and said to him, "Go, carry them to the city." And as soon as the lad was gone, David rose up from a place toward the south and fell on his face on the ground, and bowed himself three times.

They kissed one another and wept with one another, and Jonathan said to David, "Go in peace, for we have both sworn in the name of the Lord, saying, 'May the Lord be between you and me, and between your children and my children for ever.'"

David arose and departed, and Jonathan went back into the city.

DAVID SPARES SAUL'S LIFE

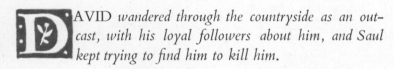

DAVID wandered through the countryside as an outcast, with his loyal followers about him, and Saul kept trying to find him to kill him.

DAVID arose one night and came to where Saul had pitched his tent, and David saw the place where Saul lay, and Abner, the son of Ner, the captain of his army, beside him. Saul lay in the middle of the camp, and his men were encamped around him.

So David took the spear and the jug of water from beside Saul's pillow, and stole away, and no man saw him or knew he was there or waked up, for they were all asleep; a deep sleep from the Lord had fallen upon them.

Then David went over to the other side and stood on the top of a hill far off, a long distance from the camp.

David cried to the people, and to Abner, the son of Ner, saying, "Are you not a courageous man? Who is like you in Israel? Why then have you not guarded the lord your king? For one of the people came in to destroy the king your lord. Look now for the king's spear and the jug of water that was at his pillow."

Then Saul knew David's voice and said, "Is that your voice, my son David?"

And David said, "It is my voice, my lord, O King." And he added, "Why does my lord pursue his servant this way? What have I done? What is the evil within me?"

Then Saul said, "I have sinned; return, my son David, for I will never more do you any harm, because my life was precious to you this day. I see now that I have been foolish and very, very wrong."

Then David went on his way, and Saul returned to his palace.

 ATER, Saul and Jonathan were both killed in battle. David then became king of Judah, and ruled for many years. After he died, his son Solomon became king.

THE PSALMS OF DAVID

(It has been thought that David wrote some of the most famous and beautiful songs of the Israelites, found in the book of Psalms.)

PSALM 23

THE Lord is my shepherd; I shall not want.
He maketh me to lie down in green pastures;
He leadeth me beside the still waters.
He restoreth my soul.
He leadeth me in the paths of righteousness
For his name's sake.
Yea, though I walk through the valley of the
    shadow of death,
I will fear no evil, for thou art with me.
Thy rod and thy staff, they comfort me.
Thou preparest a table before me in the presence
    of mine enemies;
Thou anointest my head with oil;
My cup runneth over.
Surely goodness and mercy shall follow me
All the days of my life,
And I will dwell in the house of the Lord for
    ever.

PSALM 24

The earth is the Lord's, and the fulness thereof,
The world, and they that dwell therein;
For he hath founded it upon the seas,
And established it upon the floods.

Who shall ascend into the hill of the Lord?
Or who shall stand in his holy place?
He that hath clean hands and a pure heart,
Who hath not lifted up his soul unto vanity, nor
    sworn deceitfully.

He shall receive the blessing of the Lord,
And righteousness from the God of his salvation.
This is the generation of them that seek him,
That seek thy face, O Jacob.

Lift up your heads, O ye gates,
And be ye lifted up, ye everlasting doors,
And the king of glory shall come in.

Who is this king of glory?
The Lord, strong and mighty,
The Lord, mighty in battle.

Lift up your heads, O ye gates,
Even lift them up, ye everlasting doors;
And the king of glory shall come in.

Who is this king of glory?
The Lord of hosts, he is the king of glory.

PSALM 100

Make a joyful noise unto the Lord, all ye lands.
Serve the Lord with gladness;
Come before his presence with singing.
Know ye that the Lord, he is God;
It is he that hath made us, and not we ourselves;
We are his people, and the sheep of his pasture.
Enter into his gates with thanksgiving,
And into his courts with praise;
Be thankful unto him, and bless his name.
For the Lord is good, his mercy is everlasting;
And his truth endureth to all generations.

PSALM 121

I will lift up mine eyes unto the hills,
From whence cometh my help.
My help cometh from the Lord,
Which made heaven and earth.
He will not suffer thy foot to be moved;
He that keepeth thee will not slumber.
Behold, he that keepeth Israel
Shall neither slumber nor sleep.
The Lord is thy keeper;
The Lord is thy shade upon thy right hand.
The sun shall not smite thee by day,
Nor the moon by night.
The Lord shall preserve thee from all evil;
He shall preserve thy soul.
The Lord shall preserve thy going out, and thy
    coming in,
From this time forth, and even for evermore.

93

THE WISDOM OF SOLOMON

PEOPLE of Israel in those days sacrificed on hilltops, because there was no temple built to honor the name of the Lord.

King Solomon loved the Lord and followed the laws of David his father, but he too sacrificed and burned incense on hilltops. Often the king went to Gibeon to sacrifice there, for that was the most famous hilltop; a thousand burnt offerings Solomon offered upon that altar.

In Gibeon the Lord appeared to Solomon in a dream at night, and God said, "Ask of me whatever you want."

Solomon said, "You showed great mercy to your servant David, my father, because he walked before you in truth and in righteousness, and was upright in his heart. You continued this great kindness to him in that you have given him a son to sit on his throne, as I do today.

"Now, O Lord my God, you have made your servant king instead of David my father, and I am like a little child: I do not know how to go out or come in. I am in the midst of your great people whom you have chosen, so great a people that they cannot be numbered nor counted.

"Give, therefore, to your servant an understanding heart to judge your people, that I may judge between good and bad; for who is able to judge so great a people as yours?"

God was much pleased that Solomon asked this thing. And God said to him, "Because you have asked for this thing, and have not asked for long life for yourself, nor for riches for yourself, nor for the life of your enemies, but have asked for understanding to make wise

judgments, you will see that I have done just as you asked. Lo, I have given you a wise and understanding heart, so that there has never been anyone like you before, nor shall anyone like you arise after you.

"And I have also given you that which you have not asked, both riches and honor, so that there will not be anyone who is your equal among the kings all your days.

"And if you will walk in my ways, to obey my laws and my commandments, as your father David did, then I will lengthen your days."

Then Solomon awoke and knew that it was a dream. He went to Jerusalem and stood before the ark of the covenant of the Lord, and offered up burnt offerings and peace offerings, and made a feast for all his servants.

Then there came two women to the king, and stood before him.

The one woman said, "O my lord, this woman and I live in one house, and I bore a child in the house with her. And it happened that three days afterward, this woman bore a child, too. We were together, and there was no one else in the house with the two of us.

"This woman's child died in the night because she lay upon it, and she arose at midnight and took my son from beside me, while your handmaid slept, and she took him in her arms and laid her dead child in my arms.

"And when I rose in the morning to nurse my child, I saw that it was dead; but when I had looked at it in the daylight, I found that it was not my own son."

The other woman said, "No, the living is my son and the dead is your son."

And the first woman said, "No, the dead is your son and the living is my son."

Thus they argued before the king.

Then the king said, "The one says, 'This is my son that is alive, and your son is the dead child,' and the other says, 'No, your son is the

dead one, and my son is the living.'" So the king said, "Bring me a sword," and they brought him a sword. "Divide the living child in two," he said, "and give half to the one and half to the other."

Then the mother to whom the living child belonged spoke to the king, for her heart ached for her son, and she said, "O my lord, give her the living child, and by no means kill it."

But the other said, "Let it be neither mine nor yours, but divide it."

Then the king answered and said, "Give the first woman the living child, and by no means kill it; she is the mother of it."

All Israel heard of the judgment which the king had handed down, and they respected the king. For they saw that the wisdom of God was in him, to give judgments.

And God gave Solomon great wisdom and understanding, and largeness of heart as the sand that is on the seashore. And Solomon's wisdom excelled the wisdom of all the children of the east country and all the wisdom of Egypt. For he was wiser than all men, and his fame spread through all nations round about.

And he spoke three thousand proverbs. He talked of trees, from the cedar tree that is in Lebanon even to the hyssop that springs out of the wall; he talked also of beasts, and of birds, and of creeping things, and of fish.

And people of all lands came to hear the wisdom of Solomon, from all the kings of the earth who had heard of his wisdom.

SOLOMON BUILDS THE TEMPLE

NOW *in the four hundred and eightieth year after the children of Israel had come out of the land of Egypt, in the fourth year of his reign, Solomon began to build a temple to the Lord.*

The house of the Lord which King Solomon built was ninety feet long and thirty feet broad, and the height of it was forty-five feet. There was a broad porch before the temple, and it had windows of narrow lights, and many chambers.

The house was built of stone made ready before it was brought there, so that there was no sound of a hammer or axe or any tool in the house while it was in building.

The walls and floors and ceilings of the house were of boards of cedar, and Solomon covered the floors with planks of fir.

And he covered the whole house with pure gold, and the whole altar in the holy of holies was covered with pure gold. Within the holy of holies he had two cherubims of olive wood, each fifteen feet high, and their wings touched in the middle of the room. They, too, were overlaid with gold.

All the walls and the doors were carved with cherubims and palm trees and flowers, all covered with gold, and in the inner court were three rows of stone columns, and a row of cedar beams.

Solomon had all the vessels that belonged to the house of the Lord made of gold, too; the altar was of gold, and the candlesticks of pure gold, before the holy of holies, with flowers and lamps and tongs of gold; and bowls and snuffers and basins and spoons and censers of pure gold, and hinges of gold on the doors of the temple.

The house was seven years in the building. Then the work was finished which King Solomon had done for the house of the Lord. And Solomon brought in the things which David his father had dedicated: the silver and the gold and the vessels he put among the treasures of the house of the Lord.

ELIJAH AND THE POOR WIDOW

AFTER *Solomon's reign the kingdom was divided. And it happened that one of the kings of Israel, Ahab, the son of Omri, displeased the Lord by building an altar to Baal. The Lord decided to punish him.*

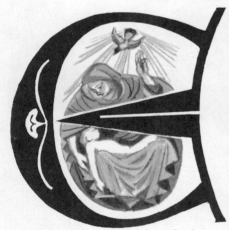

ELIJAH the Tishbite, an inhabitant of Gilead, said to Ahab, "As the Lord God of Israel lives, before whom I stand, there will not be dew nor rain for years, unless I say the word."

Then the word of the Lord came to him, saying, "Get away from here and turn eastward and hide yourself by the brook Cherith, which is this side of Jordan. There you shall drink of the brook, and I have commanded ravens to feed you there."

So he went and did as the Lord had told him, and lived by the brook Cherith. And the ravens brought him bread and meat in the morning and bread and meat in the evening, and he drank of the brook.

It came to pass, after a while, that the brook dried up, because there had been no rain in the land.

Then the word of the Lord came to him, saying, "Get up and go to Zarephath, which belongs to Zidon, and live there. You will find I have commanded a widow woman there to feed you."

So Elijah arose and went to Zarephath, and when he came to the gate of the city, he saw that the widow woman was there gathering sticks.

He called to her and said, "Fetch me, I beg of you, a little water in a vessel, so that I may have a drink." And as she was going to fetch it, he called to her and said, "Please bring me a morsel of bread."

She said, "As the Lord your God lives, I have not a loaf, but only a handful of meal in a barrel, and a little oil in a jar. As you see, I am gathering two sticks, that I may go in and prepare it for myself and my son, so that we may eat it and die."

Elijah said to her, "Do not fear; go and do as you have said; but make me a little cake of it first, and bring it to me, and afterward make some for yourself and for your son. For the Lord God of Israel has said, 'The barrel of meal shall not be empty, nor the jar of oil fail, until the day when the Lord sends rain upon the earth.'"

She went and did as Elijah told her, and she and Elijah and her household ate for many days.

But it happened, after these things, that the son of the woman, the mistress of the house, fell sick, and his sickness was so severe that there was no breath left in him.

She said to Elijah, "What have I done to you, O man of God? Have you come to me to remind me of my sins, and to kill my son?"

"Give me your son," he said to her, and he took him from her arms and carried him up to a loft where he stayed, and laid him upon his own bed.

Then he cried to the Lord and said, "O Lord my God, have you brought evil upon the widow with whom I am stopping, by killing her son?"

Then he stretched himself out upon the child three times and cried to the Lord, and said, "O Lord my God, I beg you, let this child's soul come back to him."

The Lord heard the voice of Elijah, and the soul of the child came into him again, and he breathed. Then Elijah took the child and brought him down from the chamber into the house, and gave him to his mother; and Elijah said, "See, your son lives!"

And the woman said to Elijah, "Now by this I know that you are a man of God, and that the word of the Lord which you preach is the truth."

ELIJAH AND THE PRIESTS OF BAAL

HEN King Ahab saw Elijah, Ahab said to him, "Are you the man who troubles Israel?" Elijah answered, "It is not I who have troubled Israel, but you and your father's house, by forsaking the commandments of the Lord and following Baalim.

"Now you send out and gather together all Israel at Mount Carmel, and the four hundred and fifty prophets of Baal, and the four hundred prophets of the groves who eat at Queen Jezebel's table."

So Ahab sent word to all the children of Israel and gathered the prophets together at Mount Carmel.

Then Elijah came before all the people and said, "How long will you waver between two opinions? If the Lord is God, follow him; if Baal, follow him."

The people answered not a word.

Then Elijah said to the people, "I, and I alone, remain a prophet of the Lord, but the prophets of Baal are four hundred and fifty men. Let them, then, get us two bullocks, and let them choose one bullock for themselves and cut it in pieces and lay it on the wood, but put no fire under it. And I will dress the other bullock and lay it on the wood, and put no fire under it.

"Then you call on the name of your gods, and I will call on the name of the Lord, and the God that answers with fire, let him be God."

And all the people answered and said, "It is well spoken."

Elijah said to the prophets of Baal, "Choose one bullock for yourselves and dress it first, for there are many of you. Call on the name of your gods, but do not put any fire under it."

They took the bullock which was given them, and they dressed it and called on the name of Baal from morning until noon, saying, "O Baal, hear us." But there was no voice nor any answer, though they leaped upon the altar they had made.

At noon Elijah mocked them and said, "Cry aloud for he is a god; either he is talking, or he is busy, or he is on a journey, or perhaps he is asleep and must be awakened."

They cried aloud and cut themselves, as was their custom, with knives and lances, until the blood gushed out upon their robes.

When midday was past, they worshiped before the altar until time for the evening sacrifice, and still there was neither a voice nor any answer nor any sign that their gods heard them.

Then Elijah said to all the people, "Come near to me."

All the people gathered around him. Then he walked up to the altar of the Lord which had been broken down. Elijah took twelve stones, according to the number of the tribes of the sons of Jacob which made up Israel. With the stones he built an altar in the name of the Lord, and he made a trench around the altar, large enough to hold two measures of seed. He put the wood in order, and cut the bullock in pieces and laid it on the wood.

Then he said, 'Fill four barrels with water and pour it on the burnt sacrifice and on the wood."

When they had done this he said, "Do it a second time," and they did it a second time. And he said, "Do it a third time," and they did it a third time.

The water ran around the altar, and he filled the trench with water, too.

Then, when it was time for the offering of the evening sacrifice, Elijah the prophet came near and said, "Lord God of Abraham, Isaac, and of Israel, let it be known today that you are the

God in Israel, and that I am your servant and have done all these things at your command.

"Hear me, O Lord, hear me, that this people may know that you are the Lord God, and that you may have their hearts again."

Then the fire of the Lord came down and consumed the burnt sacrifice and the wood and the stones and the dust, and licked up the water that was in the trench.

When all the people saw it, they fell on their faces and said, "The Lord, he is the God; the Lord, he is the God."

THE PARTING OF ELIJAH AND ELISHA

INALLY the Lord decided to take Elijah up into heaven in a whirlwind. At that time Elijah was with Elisha, his faithful follower. Elijah said to Elisha, "Wait here, I beg you, for the Lord has told me to go to Bethel."

But Elisha said to him, "As the Lord lives and as your soul lives, I will not leave you."

So they went down together to Bethel. Then the followers of the prophets who were at Bethel came out to meet Elisha and said to him, "Do you know that the Lord is going to take away your master from you today?"

"Yes, I know it," he said. "Hold your peace."

And Elijah said to him, "Elisha, wait here, I beg of you. For the Lord has told me to go to Jericho."

And Elisha said, "As the Lord lives, and as your soul lives, I will not leave you."

So they went on to Jericho. Then the followers of the prophets who were at Jericho came to Elisha and said to him, "Do you know that the Lord is going to take away your master from you today?"

He said, "Yes, I know it. Hold your peace."

And Elijah said to him, "Wait here, I beg you, for the Lord has told me to go to Jordan."

But Elisha said, "As the Lord lives, and as your soul lives, I will not leave you."

So the two went on. And fifty of the followers of the prophets went and stood at a distance to watch; and the two stood beside the Jordan.

Then Elijah took his mantle and folded it over, and struck the waters so that they were divided on either side, and the two men went across on dry ground.

It happened, when they had crossed over, that Elijah said to Elisha, "Ask what you will of me, before I am taken away from you."

Elisha said, "Let a double portion of your spirit be upon me, I beg of you."

"You have asked a hard thing," Elijah said. "Nevertheless, if you see me when I am taken from you, you shall have your wish; but if not, you shall not have it."

It happened, as they went on and talked together, that a chariot of fire appeared, and horses of fire, and swept them apart; and Elijah went up by a whirlwind into heaven.

Elisha saw it, and he cried, "My father, my father! The chariot of Israel, and its horsemen!" Then he could not see him any more, and he took hold of his own robe and ripped it in two.

He picked up Elijah's mantle which had fallen from him, and went back and stood by the bank of the Jordan. He took Elijah's mantle and struck the waters and said, "Where is the Lord God of Elijah?" And when he had struck the waters, they parted on either side of him, and Elisha crossed over.

When the followers of the prophets who had come to watch saw him, they said, "The spirit of Elijah rests on Elisha." And they came to meet him, and bowed themselves to the ground before him.

ELISHA CURES NAAMAN'S LEPROSY

AAMAN, captain of the army of the king of Syria, was a great man among his master's followers, and honorable. Through him the Lord had granted freedom to Syria. He was also a man of great courage; but he was a leper.

The Syrians had gone out by companies and had brought back as a captive out of the land of Israel a little girl; and she was a maidservant to Naaman's wife.

She said to her mistress, "I would to God my lord were with the prophet who is in Samaria, for he would cure him of his leprosy."

Someone went in and told the king, saying, "Thus and thus said the girl who is from the land of Israel."

The king of Syria said, "Go now, go, and I will send a letter to the king of Israel."

Naaman departed with the letter, and took with him ten talents of silver, and six thousand pieces of gold, and ten complete changes of clothing.

He delivered to the king of Israel the letter, which said: "Now when this letter comes to you, you will see that I have sent to you with it Naaman, my servant, that you may cure him of his leprosy."

When the king of Israel had read the letter, he tore his clothes, and said, "Am I God, to kill and to make alive, that this man sends a man to me to be cured of his leprosy? Perhaps he is just trying to pick a quarrel with me."

Now when Elisha the man of God heard that the king of Israel was troubled, he sent word to the king, saying, "Why did you tear your clothes? Let the man come to me, and he shall know that there is a prophet in Israel."

So Naaman came with his horses and his chariot, and stood at the door of the house of Elisha.

Elisha sent a messenger to him, saying, "Go and wash in the Jordan seven times, and your flesh shall be healed again, and you will be well."

Then Naaman was angry and went away, and said, "See now, I thought, 'He will surely come out to me and stand there and call on the name of the Lord his God and strike his hand on the place and cure the leprosy.' Are not Abana and Pharper, the rivers of Damascus, better than all the waters of Israel? May I not wash in them and be cured?"

So he turned and went away in a rage.

His servants came up and spoke to him, and said, "My father, if the prophet had ordered you to do some great thing, would you not have done it? How much rather then obey when he says to you, 'Wash and be made well'?"

Then he went down and dipped himself seven times in the Jordan, just as the man of God had said, and his flesh was once again like the flesh of a little child, and he was well.

He went back to the man of God, he and all his company, and came and stood before him, and he said, "Now I know that there is no God in all the earth but in Israel."

THE PROPHECY OF ISAIAH

AT THE time when King Uzziah died, I saw the Lord sitting on a throne lifted up on high, and his train filled the temple. Above it stood the seraphims. Each had six wings: With two he covered his face, and with two he covered his feet, and with two he did fly.

One cried to another and said, "Holy, holy, holy is the Lord of hosts. The whole earth is full of his glory."

The posts of the door moved at the voice of him who cried, and the house was filled with smoke.

Then I said, "Woe is me! For I am ruined, because I am a man of unclean lips and I dwell in the midst of people of unclean lips, and now my eyes have seen the King, the Lord of hosts."

Then one of the seraphims flew to me, bearing in his hand a live coal which he had taken from the altar with tongs. He laid it upon my mouth and said, "See, this has touched your lips, and your wickedness is taken away, and your sin purified."

Also I heard the voice of the Lord saying, "Whom shall I send? Who will go for us?"

Then I said, "Here I am. Send me."

He said, "Go and tell this people: 'You hear, but you can not understand. You see, but you can not realize what you see.'

"Make the heart of this people sluggish, and make their ears heavy, and shut their eyes, lest they see with their eyes, and hear with their ears, and understand with their hearts, and change their ways and become healed."

Then I said, "Lord, how long?"

And he answered, "Until the cities are wasted and without inhabitants, and the houses are vacant, and the land is utterly desolate. Then the Lord will have removed the men far away, and the whole land will be forsaken."

(Isaiah was one of many prophets whose outlook for the future of Israel was very gloomy, but he saw a better day coming far ahead.)

The Lord himself shall give you a king: You will see, a virgin will conceive and bear a son, and shall call his name Immanuel. Butter and honey shall he eat, that he may know how to refuse the evil and choose the good.

The people who walked in darkness have seen a great light; upon those who dwell in the land of the shadow of death, the light has shone.

For unto us a child is to be born; unto us a son shall be given. And the government shall be upon his shoulders. His name shall be called Wonderful, Counsellor, The Mighty God, The Everlasting Father, The Prince of Peace.

Of the spread of his kingdom and his peace there shall be no end, from now on, even for ever. The zeal of the Lord of hosts will bring all this about.

JOSIAH AND THE BOOK OF THE LAW

JOSIAH was eight years old when he began to rule, and he ruled thirty-one years in Jerusalem. He did what was right in the sight of the Lord, and followed in the footsteps of David his forefather, and turned not aside to the right or to the left.

It happened in King Josiah's eighteenth year that the king sent Shaphan, the son of Azaliah, the son of Meshullam, the scribe, to the house of the Lord with these words:

"Go up to Hilkiah, the high priest, and have him add up the silver which is brought into the house of the Lord, which the keepers of the door have gathered from the people. Let them deliver it into the hands of the workers who oversee the house of the Lord, and let them give it to the workers in the house of the Lord, to repair the house. Get carpenters and builders and masons, and buy timber and hewn stone to repair the temple."

No records were kept of the money that was paid to the men, because they worked faithfully.

When Shaphan the scribe went to the temple, Hilkiah the high priest said to him, "I have found the book of the law in the house of the

Lord." And Hilkiah gave the book to Shaphan, and he read it.

Shaphan the scribe came to the king and reported to the king: "Your servants have gathered up the money that was found in the temple, and have paid it to the workers who have the overseeing of the temple." Then Shaphan the scribe showed the king the book, saying, "Hilkiah the priest has delivered this book to me." And Shaphan read it before the king.

And when the king had heard the words of the book of the law (which we know as Deuteronomy), he tore his clothes, for he knew his fathers had not listened to the words of this book, to obey all the laws that were written down for them.

The king sent for all the elders of Judah and of Jerusalem; then he went up to the house of the Lord, taking all the men of Judah and all the inhabitants of Jerusalem with him, both the priests and the prophets and all the people, both small and great, and he read into their ears all the words of the book of the covenant which was found in the house of the Lord.

The king stood by a pillar and made a covenant before the Lord, to walk in his ways and to keep his commandments and follow his words and his laws, with all his heart and with all his soul, and to live up to the words of this covenant that were written in the book; and all the people stood to swear to the covenant.

Then the king commanded Hilkiah the high priest, and the priests of the second order, and the keepers of the door, to bring forth out of the temple of the Lord all the vessels that were made for Baal and his sacred wood, and for all the other gods; and he burned them outside of Jerusalem in the fields of Kidron, and carried the ashes of them to Bethel.

He put down the idolatrous priests, whom the kings of Judah had ordained to burn incense in the high places in the cities of Judah and in the places round about Jerusalem, and also those who burned incense to Baal, to the sun, and to the moon, and to the planets, and to all the various gods. Josiah destroyed also the workers with ghosts and magic, and the wizards, and the images, and the idols, and all the evil things that were to be found in the land of Judah and in Jerusalem, so that he might live up to the words of the law which were written in the book that Hilkiah the priest found in the house of the Lord.

There had been no king like Josiah. For he turned to the Lord with all his heart, and with all his soul, and with all his might, according to all the law of Moses; neither did any come after him who were his equal.

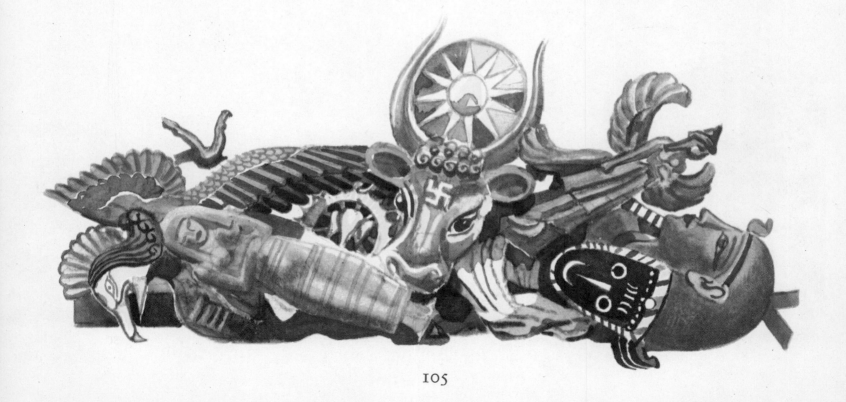

JERUSALEM IS DESTROYED

Y ET *even after Josiah, the sins of the people doomed them to be destroyed.*

D URING the ninth year of his reign, in the tenth month, on the tenth day of the month, Nebuchadnezzar, king of Babylon, came with all his Chaldean army to Jerusalem. They pitched their camp outside it and built forts facing it round about.

The city was besieged until the eleventh year of King Zedekiah's reign. And on the ninth day of the fourth month the famine spread over the city, and there was no bread for the people in the land.

The city was broken up, and the men of the army fled by night, by way of a gate between two walls, which was near the king's garden (for the Chaldeans were all around the city).

And the king went off toward the plain. The army of the Chaldeans pursued the king and overtook him on the plains of Jericho, and all his army was scattered.

So they took the king and brought him up to the king of Babylon at Riblah, and they passed judgment upon him. They bound him with fetters of brass and carried him to Babylon.

And in the fifth month, on the seventh day of the month, Nebuzaradan, captain of the guard, a servant of the king of Babylon, came to Jerusalem. He burned the house of the Lord, and the king's house, and all the houses of Jerusalem; every great man's house he burned with fire. And the army of the Chaldeans, which was with the captain of the guard, broke down the walls of Jerusalem all around the city.

The rest of the people who were left in the city, and the fugitives who fell into the hands of the king of Babylon, and the rest of the population, Nebuzaradan the captain of the guard carried away with him. But he left the poor of the land to care for the vineyards and the fields.

THE SONG OF THE CAPTIVES

By the rivers of Babylon,
There we sat down;
Yea, we wept when we remembered Zion.
We hanged our harps upon the willows
In the midst thereof.

For there they that carried us away captive
Required of us a song;
And they that wasted us
Required of us mirth, saying,
"Sing us one of the songs of Zion."

How shall we sing the Lord's song
In a strange land?

If I forget thee, O Jerusalem,
Let my right hand forget her cunning;
If I do not remember thee,
Let my tongue cleave to the roof of my mouth;
If I prefer not Jerusalem above my chief joy.

Remember, O Lord, the children of Edom
In the day of Jerusalem
Who said, "Raze it, raze it,
Even to the foundation thereof."

O daughter of Babylon
Who art to be destroyed,
Happy shall be he that rewardeth thee
As thou hast served us;
Happy shall be he that taketh and dasheth
Thy little ones against the stones.

DANIEL AT NEBUCHADNEZZAR'S COURT

HEN THE reign of Jehoiakim, king of Judah, was in its third year, Neb-uchadnezzar, king of Babylon, came to Jerusalem and besieged it. And the Lord gave Jehoia-kim, king of Judah, into his hand, with part of the vessels of the house of God; and he carried them to the land of Shinar, to the house of his gods; and the vessels he brought into the treasure house of his god.

Then the king told Ashpenaz, the master of his household, to pick certain of the children of Israel, of the king's family, and of the princes, children who had no faults but were handsome and bright and quick to learn, who understood science and had abilities worthy to stand in the king's palace; to these they would teach the wisdom and the language of the Chaldeans.

The king allowed them a daily provision of

the king's own food, and of the wine which he drank, to nourish them so that at the end of three years they might stand before the king.

Now among these were some of the children of Judah: Daniel, Hananiah, Mishael, and Azariah. To all these the master of the household gave new names; he gave Daniel the name of Belteshazzar, to Hananiah the name of Shadrach, to Mishael, Meshach, and to Azariah Abednego.

But Daniel decided in his heart that he would not pollute himself with the king's meat (which was not the food of the children of Israel) nor with the wine which he drank. Therefore he requested of the master of the household that he might not have to eat it.

Now God had filled the master of the household with love for Daniel. And the master of the household said to him, "I fear my lord the king, who has given orders for your food and drink. For why should he see your faces worse looking than the children who are in your group? If this happens, you will make me endanger my head with the king."

Then Daniel said to Melzar, whom the master of the household had put over Daniel, Hananiah, Mishael, and Azariah, "Test your servants, please, for ten days. Let them give us peas and beans to eat, and water to drink. Then look at our faces and at the faces of the children who eat some of the king's food, and then deal with your servants according to what you find."

He agreed to test them in this manner, and tried them for ten days. At the end of ten days their faces appeared fairer and plumper than any of the children who had eaten of the king's food. So Melzar took away their helpings of the meat, and the wine that they should drink, and gave them peas and beans.

As for the four children, God gave them knowledge and skill in all kinds of learning and wisdom; and Daniel had understanding of all visions and dreams.

Now at the end of the time when the king had said they should be brought in, the master of the household took them before Nebuchadnezzar.

The king talked with them, and among them all none was found like Daniel, Hananiah, Mishael, and Azariah; therefore they stayed before the king. And in all matters of wisdom and understanding in which the king tested them, he found them ten times better than all the magicians and astrologers that were in his realm.

And Daniel stayed on even until the first year of the reign of King Cyrus.

THE STATUE OF GOLD

EBUCHADNEZZAR the king made a statue of gold ninety feet high and nine feet wide. He set it up on the plain of Dura, in the land of Babylon.

Then Nebuchadnezzar the king sent out word to gather together the princes, the governors, and the captains, the judges, the treasurers, the counselors and the sheriffs, and all the rulers of the provinces, to come to see the statue.

Then the princes, the governors and captains, the judges, the treasurers, the counselors and the sheriffs, and all the rulers of the provinces gathered together to see the statue that Nebuchadnezzar the king had set up; and they stood before the statue.

Then a herald cried aloud, "To you it is commanded, O people, that when you hear the sound of the cornet, flute, harp, sackbut, psaltery, dulcimer, and all kinds of music, you shall fall down and worship the golden image that Nebuchadnezzar the king has set up. And anyone who does not fall down and worship shall in that same hour be cast into the middle of a burning fiery furnace."

Therefore when the moment came, when all the people heard the sound of the cornet, flute, harp, sackbut, psaltery, and all kinds of music, they all fell down and worshiped the golden image that Nebuchadnezzar the king had set up.

Then certain Chaldeans came up and accused the Jews. They spoke to King Nebuchadnezzar and said:

"O King, live for ever! You, O King, have sent out an order that every man who hears the sound of the cornet, flute, harp, sackbut, psaltery, and dulcimer, and all kinds of music, shall fall down and worship the golden image, and that whoever does not fall down and worship shall be cast into the middle of a burning fiery furnace.

"There are certain Jews, whom you have put in charge of the affairs of the province of Babylon. They are Shadrach, Meshach, and Abed-nego; these men, O King, have not regarded your wishes. They do not serve your gods, nor worship the golden image which you have set up."

Then Nebuchadnezzar, in his rage and fury, commanded Shadrach, Meshach, and Abednego to be brought before him.

Nebuchadnezzar said to them, "Is it true, O Shadrach, Meshach, and Abednego, that you do not serve my gods, nor worship the golden image which I have set up?

"If you are ready, when you hear the sound of the cornet, flute, harp, sackbut, psaltery and dulcimer and all kinds of music, to fall down and worship the image I have made, all is well; but if you will not worship, you will be cast, this same hour, into the middle of a burning fiery furnace; and who is the God who will deliver you out of my hands?"

Shadrach, Meshach, and Abednego answered and said to the king, "O Nebuchadnezzar, we do not need to think over our answer to you in this matter. If it be his will, our God, whom we serve, is able to save us from the burning fiery furnace, and he will save us from your hands,

O King. But if not, you must know, O King, that we still will not serve your gods, nor worship the golden image which you have set up."

Then Nebuchadnezzar was full of fury, and his face hardened against Shadrach, Meshach, and Abednego. Therefore he spoke and commanded that the furnace should be heated seven times more than usual. And he commanded the most mighty men in his army to bind Shadrach, Meshach, and Abednego, and to cast them into the burning fiery furnace.

Because the king had insisted that the furnace be exceedingly hot, the flame of the fire killed the men who led Shadrach, Meshach, and Abednego to it. But Shadrach, Meshach, and Abednego, in the midst of the burning fiery furnace, were unharmed.

Then Nebuchadnezzar the king was astonished, and rose up in haste and said to his counselors, "Did we not cast three men bound into the midst of the fire?"

They answered and said, "True, O King!"

He answered and said, "I see four men loose, walking in the midst of the fire, and they are unhurt; and the fourth looks like an angel of God."

Then Nebuchadnezzar walked up to the mouth of the burning fiery furnace and said, "Shadrach, Meshach, and Abednego, you servants of the most high God, come out and come here."

Then Shadrach, Meshach, and Abednego walked out of the fire. And all the princes, governors, and captains, and the king's counselors gathered together there and saw these men against whose bodies the fire had no power.

Not a hair of their heads was singed, nor were their clothes burnt and there was no smell of fire upon them.

Then Nebuchadnezzar spoke and said, "Blessed be the God of Shadrach, Meshach, and Abednego, who has sent his angel and saved his servants who trusted in him and who defied the king's word and risked their lives that they might not serve or worship any god except their own God.

"Therefore I make a decree: Any people, nation, or group who say anything against the God of Shadrach, Meshach, and Abednego, shall be cut in pieces, and their houses shall be made a dumping ground; for there is no other god who can save in this way."

Then the king promoted Shadrach, Meshach, and Abednego to high offices in the province of Babylon.

THE HANDWRITING ON THE WALL

UPON the death of Nebuchadnezzar, his son Belshazzar became king. Belshazzar gave a great feast for a thousand of his lords and drank wine before the thousand. While he tasted the wine, Belshazzar commanded servants to bring the golden and silver vessels which his father Nebuchadnezzar had taken out of the temple which was in Jerusalem, so that the king and his princes, his wives, and the other women of his house might drink from them.

They brought the golden vessels that were taken out of the temple of the house of God, and his princes, his wives, and the other women drank from them. They drank wine and praised the gods of gold, and of silver, of brass, of iron, of wood, and of stone.

Within the same hour there appeared the fingers of a man's hand, writing upon the wall of the king's palace; and the king saw the part of the hand that wrote.

Then the king's face changed, and his thoughts troubled him so that the joints of his legs were loose and his knees knocked together.

The king cried aloud to bring in the astrologers, the Chaldeans, and the soothsayers, and the king said to these wise men of Babylon, "Whoever reads this writing and tells me the meaning of it shall be clothed in scarlet, and have a chain of gold about his neck, and shall be the third ruler in the country."

All the king's wise men came in, but they could not read the writing nor make known to the king the meaning of it.

Then King Belshazzar was greatly troubled, and his face changed, and his lords were dazed.

Now the queen, called by the king and his lords, came into the banqueting room, and the queen spoke and said, "O King, live forever! Do not let your thoughts trouble you, nor let your face change. There is a man in your kingdom who has in him the spirit of the holy gods. In the days of your father, light and understanding and wisdom like the wisdom of the gods was found in him. The king, Nebuchadnezzar, your father, made him master of the magicians, astrologers, Chaldeans and soothsayers because of his excellent spirit and the knowledge and understanding, interpreting of dreams, explaining of hard sentences, and clearing up of doubts which Daniel, whom the king named Belteshazzar, accomplished. Now let Daniel be called, and he will tell you the meaning of this."

Then Daniel was brought in before the king, and the king said to Daniel, "Are you that Daniel who is one of the children of the captivity of Judah, whom the king my father brought out of the land of the Jews? I have heard of you, that the spirit of the gods is in you, and that light and understanding and excellent wisdom are found in you.

"Now the wise men and astrologers have been brought in before me to read this writing and tell me the meaning of it, but they could not interpret it for me. I have heard of you, and that you can give interpretations and clear up meanings. Now if you can read the writing and make the meaning of it clear to me, you shall be clothed in scarlet and have a chain of gold around your neck, and you shall be the third ruler in the kingdom."

Then Daniel answered and said to the king, "Keep your gifts for yourself and give your rewards to someone else, but I will read the writing to the king and tell him the meaning of it.

"O King, the most high God gave Nebuchadnezzar, your father, a kingdom and majesty and glory and honor. And because of the majesty that he gave him all people, nations, and languages trembled and feared him—he killed whom he wanted to and kept alive whom he wanted to and raised men up or put them down as he liked. But when his heart was lifted up and his mind hardened in pride, his kingly throne was taken from him, and his glory was taken from him, until he knew that the most high God ruled in the kingdom of men, and that he chooses to rule over it whomever he wishes.

"And you his son, O Belshazzar, have not kept your heart simple, though you knew all this, but you have lifted yourself up against the Lord of heaven. They have brought you the vessels of his house, and you and your lords, your wives and other women have drunk wine in them, and you have praised the gods of silver and gold, of brass, iron, wood, and stone, which do not see nor hear nor know; and the God in whose hands your breath of life is and whose ways should be yours, you have not praised.

"This hand, then, was sent from him, and the writing was written by his hand. And this is the writing that was written:

MENE, MENE, TEKEL, PERES.

"This is the meaning of the thing: MENE, God has judged your kingdom and finished it; TEKEL, you have been weighed in the scales and found lacking; PERES, your kingdom will be divided and given to the Medes and Persians."

Then Belshazzar commanded that they clothe Daniel in scarlet and put a chain of gold about his neck; and he made a proclamation saying that he was to be the third ruler in the kingdom.

That night Belshazzar the king of the Chaldeans was killed. And Darius, the Mede, took the kingdom.

DANIEL IN THE LIONS' DEN

IT PLEASED Darius to set over the kingdom a hundred and twenty princes who were to rule the whole kingdom. And over these were three presidents, and of them Daniel was the first. The princes were to give account to them, so that the king would not have any troubles.

Daniel was put over the presidents and princes because of his excellent mind; and the king planned to put him over the whole kingdom. Then the presidents and princes tried to find some fault with Daniel concerning the kingdom, but they could find no fault, because he was faithful, and there was no error or fault to be found in him.

Then these men said, "We shall not find any grounds for complaint against Daniel except that he follows the laws of his God."

Then these presidents and princes assembled together before the king and said to him, "King Darius, live forever! All the presidents of the kingdom, and the governors and the princes, the counselors and the captains, have consulted together about establishing a royal law, by a firm order, that whoever asks anything of any god or man for thirty days, except of you, O King, shall be cast into the den of lions.

"Now, O King, establish this order, and sign the writing, that it may not be changed, according to the law of the Medes and the Persians, which does not change."

Then King Darius signed the writing.

Now when Daniel knew that the law was signed, he went into his house and, his windows being open in his chamber facing Jerusalem, he kneeled down three times a day and prayed and gave thanks to his God, just as he had before.

Then the men came together and found Daniel praying and entreating God. They hurried to the king and reminded him of his order.

"Did you not sign an order that any man asking a favor of any god or man within thirty days, except yourself, O King, shall be thrown into the den of lions?"

The king answered and said, "That is true, according to the law of the Medes and the Persians, which does not change."

Then they answered and said to the king, "That Daniel, who is one of the children of the captivity of Judah, does not respect you, O King, nor the order which you have signed, but makes his requests three times a day."

When he heard these words, the king was very much displeased with himself, and he set his heart on saving Daniel. He thought until the setting of the sun about how to save Daniel.

Then the men came before the king and said to him, "Remember, O King, that it is the law of the Medes and Persians that no order or law

which the king lays down can be changed."

Then the king commanded them to take Daniel and throw him into the den of lions. And the king said to Daniel, "Your God, whom you serve so faithfully, surely he will save you."

Then a stone was brought and laid across the mouth of the den; and the king sealed it with his own signet, and with the signet of his lords, so that the plan might not be changed concerning Daniel.

Then the king went to his palace and passed the night in fasting. No musical instruments were brought in to him, and he did not sleep at all.

Very early in the morning the king arose and hurried to the den of lions. When he came to the den, he cried out in a sorrowing voice to Daniel and said to him, "O Daniel, servant of the living God, has your God, whom you serve

so faithfully, been able to save you from the lions?"

Then Daniel said to the king, "O King, live forever. My God has sent his angel and has shut the lions' mouths, so that they have not hurt me, because I was innocent in his sight; and I have done no harm to you either, O King."

Then the king was exceedingly glad for him, and commanded that Daniel should be brought up out of the den. So Daniel was brought up out of the den, and no kind of wound was found on him, because he had believed firmly in his God.

Then the king gave commands, and they brought the men who had accused Daniel, and they cast them into the den of lions, and their children and their wives, too. And the lions broke all their bones into pieces.

Then King Darius wrote to all people and nations, and in all the languages of all the earth:

"Peace be multiplied to you! I now command that in every part of my kingdom men tremble and fear before the God of Daniel, for he is the living God, unchanging forever, and his kingdom shall never be destroyed, and his power shall continue to the end. He rescues and saves, and he works signs and wonders in heaven and on earth, he who has saved Daniel from the power of the lions."

So Daniel prospered in the reign of Darius, and in the reign of Cyrus the Persian.

THE TEMPLE IS REBUILT

SO THAT the word of the Lord might be fulfilled, the Lord stirred up the spirit of Cyrus, King of Persia, so that in the first year of his reign he sent out a notice throughout all his kingdom and put it into writing, saying:

"Thus says Cyrus, King of Persia: The Lord God of Heaven has given me all the kingdoms of the earth, and he has ordered me to build him a house at Jerusalem, which is in Judah.

"Who is there among you who are of his people? May his God be with him, and let him go up to Jerusalem, which is in Judah, and build the house of the Lord God of Israel in Jerusalem.

"And whoever remains in any place where he stops, let the men of that place help him with silver and with goods and with beasts, besides the freewill offering for the house of God in Jerusalem."

Then up rose the chief of the leaders of Judah and Benjamin, and the priests and the Levites, with all those whose spirits God had raised, to go to build the house of the Lord in Jerusalem.

And all who were around them filled their hands with vessels of silver, with gold, with goods of all sorts, with beasts, and with precious things, besides all the free offerings.

And Cyrus the king brought out the vessels of the house of the Lord which Nebuchadnezzar had brought out of Jerusalem and had put in the house of his gods.

When the seventh month was past, and the children of Israel were back in their cities, the people gathered together in Jerusalem.

And when the builders laid the foundation of the temple of the Lord, they set the priests in their robes with trumpets, and the Levites with cymbals, to praising the Lord, after the order of David, King of Israel.

And they sang together, praising and giving thanks to the Lord, because he is good, and his mercy toward Israel endures for ever. And all the people shouted with a great shout when they praised the Lord, because the foundation of the house of the Lord was laid.

ESTHER SAVES HER PEOPLE

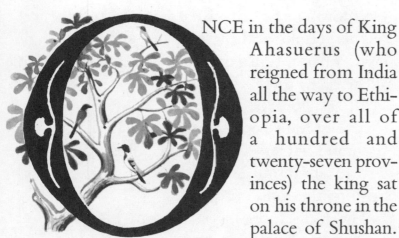

ONCE in the days of King Ahasuerus (who reigned from India all the way to Ethiopia, over all of a hundred and twenty-seven provinces) the king sat on his throne in the palace of Shushan. There were white, green, and blue hangings, fastened with cords of fine linen and purple. cloth to silver rings and pillars of marble. The beds were of gold and silver, upon a pavement of red and blue and white and black marble.

Now in the palace there was a certain Jew, whose name was Mordecai, the son of Jair, the son of Shimei, the son of Kish, a Benjamite. He had been carried away from Jerusalem with the captives whom Nebuchadnezzar, the king of Babylon, had carried away.

He brought up Hadassah, his uncle's daughter, who was called Esther because she had no father or mother. The girl was fair and beautiful, and when her father and mother died, Mordecai took her for his own daughter.

The king loved Esther above all the women, and she pleased him more than all the other maidens; so he set the royal crown upon her head and made her queen.

Now in those days, while Mordecai sat at the king's gate, two of the king's chamberlains, Bigthan and Teresh, two of those who guarded the door, were angry and tried to harm King Ahasuerus.

The plot was known to Mordecai, who told

it to Esther the queen, and Esther told the king of it in Mordecai's name. When the matter was investigated, it was found true, and the men were both hanged on a tree; and it was written in the king's book of the events of the day.

Now it happened that King Ahasuerus promoted a man named Haman, son of Hammedatha the Agagite, to a position above all the princes who worked with him. All the king's servants who were within the king's gate bowed down before Haman, for the king had commanded that this should be done. But Mordecai did not bow nor show him respect.

And when Haman saw that Mordecai did not bow nor do him reverence, then Haman was full of anger. And he scorned to lay hands on Mordecai alone, for he had been told to what people Mordecai belonged. Therefore Haman wanted to destroy all the Jews who lived throughout the whole kingdom of Ahasuerus, all the people of Mordecai.

Haman said to King Ahasuerus, "There is a certain people scattered abroad and spread among the people in all the provinces of your kingdom. Their laws are different from the rest of the people, and they do not keep the king's laws. Therefore it is not to the king's benefit to allow them there.

"If it pleases the king, let a law be written that they may be destroyed, and I will pay ten thousand talents of silver to those who take charge of the business so that this money will go into the king's treasuries."

The king took his ring from his hand and gave it to Haman, the son of Hammedatha the Agagite, the enemy of the Jews.

The king said to Haman, "The silver is yours, and the people too, to do with them whatever seems good to you."

Then the king's scribes were called on the thirteenth day of the first month, and an order was written, as Haman dictated, to the king's lieutenants, and to the governors of all the provinces, and to the rulers of the people of every province, each in their own writing, and to each people in their language; all in the name of King Ahasuerus it was written and sealed with the king's ring.

Then the letters were sent by post into all the king's provinces, telling people to kill all Jews, both young and old, little children and women, in one day, on the thirteenth day of the twelfth month, which is the month Adar; and their belongings were to be taken as spoils.

When Mordecai learned all that had been done, he tore his clothes and put on sackcloth with ashes, and went out into the midst of the city, and cried with a loud and bitter cry.

Esther's maids and her chamberlain came and told this to her. Then the queen was exceedingly sad. She called for Hatach, one of the king's chamberlains, whom he had appointed to wait on her, and gave him a message to Mordecai, asking what was wrong.

So Hatach went out to Mordecai in the street of the city which ran before the king's gate. And Mordecai told him of all that had happened, and of the sum of money that Haman had promised to pay to the king's treasuries for destroying the Jews. Also he gave him a copy of the written decree that was given out in Shushan for destroying them, to show it to Esther and tell her to go in to the king and plead with him for her people.

Hatach came and told Esther of Mordecai's words.

Again Esther spoke to Hatach and gave him a message for Mordecai: "All the king's servants and the people of the king's provinces know that if anyone, whether man or woman, who has not been called shall come before the king in the inner court, the king has a law to put him to death. Only if the king shall hold out the golden sceptre, he may live; but I have not been called to come in before the king for thirty days."

They told Mordecai of Esther's words, and Mordecai sent Esther his answer: "Do not think that you will escape, in the king's house, any more than the rest of the Jews. If you hold your peace now, release and deliverance will come to the Jews from some other quarter, but you and your father's house will be destroyed, and who knows whether you have not been sent to the kingdom for just such a time as this?"

Then Esther bade them take back to Mordecai this answer: "Go, gather together all the Jews who live in Shushan, and fast for me, neither eating nor drinking, for three days, night and day. My maidens and I will fast likewise, and then I will go in to the king, which is not according to the law. And if I perish, I perish."

So Mordecai went his way and did all that Esther commanded him.

On the third day, Esther put on her royal robes and stood in the inner court of the king's house, close beside the king's house, and the king sat upon his royal throne in the royal house, on the side near the gate of the house.

It happened that, when the king saw Esther the queen standing in the court, she won his favor; and the king held out to Esther the golden sceptre that was in his hand. So Esther drew near and touched the top of the sceptre.

Then the king said to her, "What would you like, Queen Esther? What is your request? It shall be given you, even to half of the kingdom."

And Esther answered, "If it seems good to the king, let the king and Haman come today to the banquet I have prepared for them."

So the king and Haman came to banquet with Esther the queen. And the king said again to Esther at the banquet of wine, "What is your desire, Queen Esther? It shall be granted you. What is your request? It shall be done, even to half of the kingdom."

Then Esther the queen answered and said, "If I have found favor in your sight, O King, and if it please the king, let my life be given me at my desire, and my people be saved at my request. For we are sold, my people and I, to be destroyed, to be slain, to perish."

Then King Ahasuerus answered and said to Esther the queen, "Who is he and where is he who dares presume in his heart to do this?"

And Esther said, "The foe and enemy is the wicked Haman."

Then Haman was afraid before the king and the queen.

And Harbonah, one of the chamberlains, said to the king, "Behold, there is the gallows, seventy-five feet high, which Haman has made for Mordecai, who spoke up well for the king once. It stands in the house of Haman."

Then the king said, "Hang him on it."

So they hanged Haman on the gallows that he had prepared for Mordecai. Then the king's anger was quieted.

On that day King Ahasuerus gave the house of Haman, the enemy of the Jews, to Esther the queen, and he sent out orders to spare the Jews. And Mordecai came before the king, for Esther had told what relation he was to her.

The king took off his ring, which he had taken back from Haman, and gave it to Mordecai. And Mordecai went out from the presence of the king in royal robes of blue and white, and with a great crown of gold, and with a garment of fine linen and purple; and the city of Shushan rejoiced and was glad.

And the Jews had light and gladness, and joy and honor.